new Asian cooking

The Confident Cooking Promise of Success

Welcome to the world of Confident Cooking,
where recipes are double-tested by our team
of home economists to achieve a high standard
of success—and delicious results every time.

bay books

AF584621

C O N T E

Fried Rice, page 59

Spring Rolls, page 44

Stir-Fried Chicken with Lemon Grass, Ginger and Chilli, page 48

Fried Noodles, page 31

N T S

Musaman Beef Curry, page 16

Sago Pudding, page 110

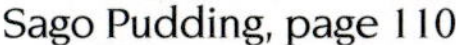

The Publisher thanks the following for their assistance in the photography for this book: Steve Costi Seafoods Pty Ltd, North Sydney; Paddington Fine Foods

Prawn and Vegetable Tempura, page 34

Tom Yum Goong, page 12

The test kitchen where our recipes are double-tested by our team of home economists to achieve a high standard of success and delicious results every time.

When we test our recipes, we rate them for ease of preparation. The following cookery ratings are on the recipes in this book, making them easy to use and understand.

A single Cooking with Confidence symbol indicates a recipe that is simple and generally quick to make —perfect for beginners.

Two symbols indicate the need for just a little more care and a little more time.

Three symbols indicate special dishes that need more investment in time, care and patience—but the results are worth it.

Glossary of Ingredients

Some of the ingredients essential for creating the authentic flavours of Asia may seem daunting at first. However, specialist Asian food stockists are now widespread, making it easy to acquire the more unusual herbs, spices and vegetables and experiment with them.

ANNATTO SEEDS
Small red triangular-shaped seeds with a subtle flavour and vivid colour. Used extensively in Latin American cooking, they were introduced to the Philippines by the Spanish traders. Once they have been fried in oil, the seeds are usually removed and the coloured oil is used in the dish. Annatto seeds are used by the Chinese to colour their roast pork.

ASIAN SHALLOTS
Small reddish/purple onions, commonly used in Asian cookery. These grow in bulbs, like garlic, and are sold in segments that look like large cloves of garlic. They have a concentrated flavour and are easy to slice and grind. If necessary, use red onions as a substitute — one small red onion to 4–6 Asian shallots.

BANANA LEAVES
Large, pliable green leaves from the banana tree, used throughout Asia as disposable plates and platters, as well as for wrapping food that is to be baked or steamed. Before use, remove the centre stalk, rinse the leaves in cold water and then blanch briefly in boiling water, to soften. Available in packets from Asian food stores if you don't have access to fresh.

BASIL
Thai Basil has a strong aroma and is used extensively in Asian cooking. The green and purple serrated-edged leaves branch from a purple stem. The flowers are pink. The leaves are added to Thai curries and stir-fries at the end of cooking. The Vietnamese use it as a garnish for soups.
Lemon Basil, as the name implies, has a mild lemon flavour. It is sprinkled over salads and soups. The leaves resemble Thai Basil, but don't have the purple tinge.

BEAN SPROUTS
Used mainly in salads and as a stir-fry vegetable, soya bean sprouts are crunchy, white, short sprouts. Discard any that are limp or brown. They are highly perishable so use within three days of purchase. Traditionally, the scraggly ends are removed.

CANDLENUTS
Large, cream-coloured nuts, similar to macadamias in shape but with a drier texture. They cannot be eaten raw as the oil is thought to be toxic. They are ground and used to thicken curries and sauces.

CHILLIES
Bird's eye are the hottest chillies of all. From 1–3 cm ($\frac{1}{2}$–$1\frac{1}{4}$ inches) long, they are available fresh, dried or pickled in brine.
Small red chillies, approximately 5 cm (2 inches) long, are the chillies used to make chilli powder and chilli flakes. Most commonly used in Thai cooking.
Medium chillies, 10–15 cm (4–6 inches) long, are most commonly used in Indonesian and Malaysian cooking. They are a thin chilli and are hot, but not overpowering. The seeds are the hottest part.
Large red and green chillies, 15–20 cm (6–8 inches) long, these thick chillies are used in Northern Thai cooking. The ripe red chillies are fiery.

To avoid skin irritation, take great care when seeding or chopping chillies — wear rubber gloves. After handling chillies, don't touch your face, eyes or any tender part of the body and always wash your hands thoroughly. If you like a hot curry, leave the seeds in, but if you prefer a milder flavour, discard the seeds.

Whole chillies freeze well in plastic bags and can be chopped while still frozen. Some chillies are available dried and are usually soaked in water, to soften, before use.

CHINESE DRIED MUSHROOMS
These impart a very distinct flavour to the dish and are used in Asian dishes that have a Chinese influence. Store them in a sealed container in a cool place. They need to be soaked before use.

CORIANDER
Also known as cilantro, coriander is the most common herb used in Thai cooking. The whole plant is used — the root, stem, seeds and leaves. The seeds are roasted and then ground in a spice mill and used in curry pastes. Fresh coriander is available from Asian food stores, greengrocers, or in pots from plant nurseries. The leaves are used for their fresh, peppery flavour, and as a garnish. For storage, wash and dry the fresh herbs before placing them in plastic bags in the refrigerator — they will keep for 5–6 days. Dried coriander is not a suitable substitute.

CRISP FRIED ONION AND GARLIC
Finely sliced garlic cloves or onions that have been deep-fried until crisp. If you don't want to make your own, you can buy them in packets. They are added to soups, noodle dishes or salads just before serving.

CURRY LEAVES
Curry leaves are used a lot in Asian cooking, especially vegetable curries, to impart a distinctive flavour. They are small, pointed leaves with a spicy fragrance and are available fresh from greengrocers, or dried from Asian grocery stores. Use as you would bay leaves and remove before serving.

DAIKON
Large white radish, used extensively in Japan. It is grated or thinly sliced for use as a garnish, or pickled in a solution of soy sauce and sugar. Available fresh, or packaged as a pickle.

DASHI
Basic stock in Japanese cuisine. Made with dried kelp and dried bonito (a fish). Available packaged in ground form, as granules or in flakes — simply add hot water to make up stock.

DRIED SHRIMP
Tiny, salted shrimp that have been dried in the sun. These are used for flavour, especially in sauces.

FISH SAUCE
This brown, salty sauce with a characteristic 'fishy' smell is an important ingredient in Thai and Vietnamese cookery. It is made from small fish that have been fermented in the sun for a long time.

GALANGAL
Related to ginger and quite similar-looking, but it is pinkish and has a distinct peppery flavour. Used in curry pastes, stir-fries and soups. Use fresh galangal, if possible, and be careful when handling that you don't get the juice on your clothes or hands, as it stains. Dried galangal must be soaked in hot water before use. Galangal powder is also known as Laos powder.

GINGER
A delicious, aromatic ingredient, important in Asian cooking. Fresh ginger is readily available — buy firm, unwrinkled rhizomes and store them in a plastic bag so they don't dry out.

GREEN PAWPAW
Commonly used in Asian salads and some soups, or as a snack with sugar and chilli — these are not a different variety but are underripe pawpaw. To shred the green pawpaw, peel it and slice it finely. It is sometimes blanched lightly before shredding.

KAFFIR LIMES AND LEAVES
A knobbly, dark-skinned lime with a very strong lime fragrance and flavour. The leaves are finely shredded for use in curry pastes and salads, or added whole to curries. The rind is also very pungent and is grated over salads, soups and curries.

KECAP MANIS
A thick, sweet soy sauce that is widely used in Indonesian and Malaysian cooking as a seasoning or sauce for satays.

LEMON GRASS
An aromatic fresh herb that is used in curry pastes, stir-fries and soups. The stems can be up to 60 cm (2 feet) long. Trim the base, remove the tough, outer layers and finely slice, chop or pound the white interior. For pastes and salads, use the tender, white portion just above the root. The whole stem, trimmed and washed thoroughly, can be added to simmering soups and curries and removed before serving. Dried lemon grass is available and needs to be soaked in water for half an hour before use. However, the flavour of fresh is superior.

MIRIN
A mild, low-alcohol form of sake, this rice cooking wine lends sweetness to sauces, grilled dishes and glazes.

MISO
A thick, fermented paste, made from soya beans and other ingredients, including wheat and rice. Available in many varieties including light brown, red, brown, yellow and white, each differing in flavour and texture. Used in soups, sauces, marinades and dips.

NOODLES

Hokkien noodles are wheat flour noodles that have been cooked and lightly oiled before packaging. They need no preparation before use — simply stir-fry or add to soups or salads. Originally from China but now found throughout Asia in Thai, Malaysian and Singaporean cuisine. They are yellow and have a rubbery texture. Refrigerate in the packet until ready to use. Asian brands are a better quality. Also known and sold as Fukkien and Singapore noodles.

Fresh egg noodles are made from egg and wheat flour. They need to be cooked in boiling water before use. Traditionally used in chow mein and short soups, they are now widely used in Asian recipes. Sold in a variety of widths, the most common being the thin angel hair. They are a soft yellow and are dusted lightly with flour before being packaged. Refrigerate in the packet until ready to use.

Fresh rice noodles are white rice noodles that have been steamed and lightly oiled before packaging. They are sold, ready to use, in packets. They come in thick or thin noodles or in a sheet that can be cut to the desired width.

Fresh rice spaghetti also known as **Laksa noodles**, are fresh, round, white rice noodles that resemble cooked spaghetti. If not readily available, use dried rice vermicelli.

Dried rice sticks are translucent flat noodles that resemble fettucine. They need to be soaked in warm water before using. Used mainly in

stir-fries, but can be used in soups and salads. Sold packaged in bundles.

Dried rice vermicelli are thin translucent noodles, sold packaged in blocks. They need to be soaked in boiling water or boiled until tender and drained thoroughly before use. Sometimes used as a garnish, the dried rice vermicelli is deep-fried until it expands.

Dried mung bean vermicelli (cellophane noodles) are thread-like translucent noodles made from mung beans. Most recipes call for them to be soaked in warm water before using, but they can be cooked in boiling water until tender. They are sold packaged in bundles and a little goes a long way. After opening, store in an airtight container.

Dried potato starch noodles are fine, green-brown, translucent noodles, about 32 cm (13 inches) long. Cook in a large pan of rapidly boiling water for 5 minutes, rinse and drain well. Once cooked, they are plump and gelatinous. Overcooking will cause them to break down and become gluggy. Also known as Korean vermicelli.

Soba are noodles made from buckwheat flour and available dried, and sometimes fresh.

Dried udon noodles are white, Japanese wheat flour noodles, that are round or flat. They are usually added to miso soup, or cooked in boiling water before use.

Fresh udon noodles are very popular and if available should be used in preference to the dried.

Shanghai noodles are fresh, white wheat flour noodles that need to be cooked in boiling water before use. Available in thick or thin, they are dusted lightly in flour before packing. Thick fresh egg noodles are sometimes called Shanghai noodles.

NORI

The most common form of dried seaweed used by the Japanese and Koreans. It comes in sheets or soft shreds, plain or roasted (for a more palatable flavour). Additional quick toasting over a naked flame freshens the nori and produces a nutty flavour.

PALM SUGAR

Obtained from either the palmyra palm or sugar palm and available in block form or in jars. The colour ranges from pale golden to very dark brown. Palm sugar is thick and crumbly and can be gently melted or grated before adding to sauces or dressings. Soft brown sugar, demerara sugar, or coconut sugar can be substituted, if necessary.

PANDAN LEAVES

Also known as screw pine, the long, flat leaves are used for flavour and colour in Asian cooking. Before adding to the dish, partly shred and tie in a knot to hold together. Available in dried form but fresh leaves give a more intense flavour. Essence is used to flavour Asian desserts.

PICKLED GINGER

Fresh, thin, pink or white slices of ginger preserved in brine. Used in rice dishes and as a garnish. A good palate cleanser with a very sharp flavour.

RICE

Jasmine is a long-grain, fragrant white rice used throughout Southeast Asia. Usually steamed or cooked using the absorption method, and then served as an accompaniment to many Asian meals.

Black glutinous is a long-grain rice used for Asian desserts and snacks. It has a sticky texture when cooked, a quality many people enjoy. Normally soaked before boiling.

White glutinous also becomes a little sticky when cooked. Soak before steaming. Usually served as a dessert, but some Asian countries use it as an accompaniment to savoury dishes instead of white long-grain.

RICE FLOUR

This is used to thicken sauces and curries or bind meat mixtures. It is also used in desserts. Cornflour can be substituted, but doesn't impart the same texture.

RICE PAPER WRAPPERS

Clear, flat, brittle rounds of paper that need to be soaked or brushed lightly with cold water to make them pliable. Available in large or small, they are used to enclose sweet or savoury fillings.

RICE VINEGAR

A mild, sweet, delicately flavoured vinegar made from rice.

SAKE

Rice wine, available in differing strengths, for cooking or drinking. Cooking sake has a lower alcohol content.

SESAME OIL

A very aromatic oil, made from roasted sesame seeds. Used in Thai recipes that have a Chinese influence. Use it sparingly as it has quite a strong, rich flavour and a little goes a long way.

SESAME AND SEAWEED SPRINKLE

A combination of finely chopped nori, roasted sesame seeds and salt. Sprinkle on noodles, salads and egg dishes.

SHOSHOYU (Japanese Soy Sauce)

This is much lighter and sweeter than Chinese soy sauce and not thick like kecap manis. It is naturally brewed, so refrigerate after opening.

SHRIMP PASTE, DRIED (Blachan)

Made from prawns or shrimps that have been dried, salted and pounded into blocks. This has a pungent smell and, once opened, should be sealed in an airtight container in the refrigerator. It should always be roasted or fried before adding to a recipe. Also known as belaccin, terasi, kapi.

SHRIMP PASTE/SAUCE (Bagoong)

Shrimps or prawns that have been salted and fermented in earthenware pots. Used as a condiment and an ingredient.

SNAKE BEANS

Long, deep green, stringless beans which grow up to 30 cm (12 inches). Cut in short lengths, they are used in stir-fries, curries and sometimes soups.

SPRING ROLL WRAPPERS

Paper-thin wrappers, available fresh or frozen, used to make many wrapped snacks including spring rolls. Defrost frozen wrappers before use.

TAMARIND CONCENTRATE

Available in a variety of forms, but commonly as concentrate, this fibrous pod is used to give an acidic effect to dishes.

TOFU

A milky-white soya bean curd, available in very firm or soft (silken) blocks. Also available in fried puffs. With a subtle taste, tofu absorbs the flavours of spices and sauces.

TONKATSU SAUCE

A tasty barbecue-style sauce made with tomatoes, apples, Japanese Worcestershire sauce and mustard. Usually served with breaded fried pork.

TURMERIC

A bitter spice used for its intense, bright yellow-orange colour. This is an ingredient in many curry powders. If you use the fresh root, peel away the skin and finely grate the flesh.

VIETNAMESE MINT

Eaten raw in salads or as an accompaniment to most Vietnamese dishes, this has a flavour that resembles coriander, but is slightly sharper.

WASABI

A pungent paste made from the root of the wasabi (horseradish) plant. This is extremely hot, so use with discretion. It is available as a powder or a paste.

THAILAND

BEEF SALAD

Preparation time: 35 minutes
Total cooking time: 10 minutes
Serves 4

3 cloves garlic, finely chopped
4 coriander roots, finely chopped
1/2 teaspoon freshly ground black pepper
3 tablespoons oil
400 g (12 2/3 oz) piece rump or sirloin steak
1 small soft-leaved lettuce
200 g (6 1/2 oz) cherry tomatoes
1 medium Lebanese cucumber
4 spring onions
1/2 cup (15 g/1/2 oz) fresh coriander leaves

Dressing
2 tablespoons fish sauce
2 tablespoons lime juice
1 tablespoon soy sauce
2 teaspoons chopped fresh red chillies
2 teaspoons soft brown sugar

1 Combine the chopped garlic and coriander roots, black pepper and 2 tablespoons of the oil. If you have a mortar and pestle, use it to finely grind the mixture. Alternatively, blend the mixture well in a food processor or blender. Spread the mixture evenly over the steak.

2 Heat the remaining oil in a heavy-based frying pan or wok over high heat. Add the steak to the pan and cook for about 4 minutes each side, turning the steak once only during the cooking time. Remove the steak from the pan and allow to cool.

3 Meanwhile, wash the lettuce and separate the leaves, cut the cherry tomatoes in half, cut the cucumber into chunks and chop the spring onions.

4 To make Dressing: Combine the fish sauce, lime juice, soy sauce, chopped red chillies and brown sugar in a small bowl, stirring until the sugar has dissolved.

5 Cut the cooled steak into thin strips. Arrange the prepared lettuce on a serving plate and arrange the cherry tomatoes over the top, with the cucumber, spring onion and strips of steak. Drizzle with the dressing and scatter the fresh coriander leaves over the top. Serve immediately.

COOK'S FILE

Hint: Be careful that you don't overcook the steak — it should be pink and, therefore, succulent and tender.

Note: Ground herbs and spices are used extensively for flavouring in Asian cookery. Small amounts can be done with a mortar and pestle or a clean coffee grinder. For larger quantities, use a blender or food processor. To help clean the bowl after grinding spices, run some stale bread through the processor.

Grind the garlic, coriander roots, black pepper and oil in a mortar and pestle.

When the steak has cooled, use a sharp knife to cut it into thin strips.

TOD MAN PLA
(Thai Fish Cakes)

Preparation time: 30 minutes
Total cooking time: 10 minutes
Serves 4–6

450 g ($14\frac{1}{3}$ oz) firm white boneless fish fillets
3 tablespoons rice flour or cornflour
1 tablespoon fish sauce
1 egg, beaten
$\frac{1}{2}$ cup (15 g/$\frac{1}{2}$ oz) fresh coriander leaves
3 teaspoons red curry paste
1–2 teaspoons chopped red chillies, optional
100 g ($3\frac{1}{3}$ oz) green beans, very finely sliced
2 spring onions, finely chopped
$\frac{1}{2}$ cup (125 ml/4 fl oz) oil, for frying
dipping sauce (see page 100) or bottled sweet chilli sauce

1 Process the fish in a food processor for 20 seconds or until smooth. Add the rice flour, fish sauce, beaten egg, coriander leaves, curry paste and chillies, if using. Process for 10 seconds or until well combined. Transfer the fish mixture to a large bowl. Add the green beans and spring onion and mix thoroughly.

2 Using wet hands, form 2 tablespoons of mixture at a time into flattish patties.

3 Heat the oil in a heavy-based frying pan over medium heat. Cook 4 fish cakes at a time until they are golden brown on both sides. Drain on paper towels and serve immediately, with a dipping sauce.

COOK'S FILE

Note: Freshly made curry pastes (page 101) give the best flavour.

Process the fish fillets in a food processor until they have a smooth texture.

Wet your hands and form patties, using 2 tablespoons of mixture at a time.

Cook the fish cakes over medium heat until golden on both sides.

SPICY CHILLI PRAWNS

Preparation time: 25 minutes
+ 10 minutes marinating
Total cooking time: 10 minutes
Serves 4

500 g (1 lb) raw prawns
2 tablespoons red curry paste
2 tablespoons oil
2 limes
2 tablespoons shredded pickled ginger

1 Peel the prawns, leaving the tails intact. Gently pull out the large back vein (but do not cut down the back). A small skewer or tweezers make it easy to remove the vein.

2 Combine the prawns, curry paste and 1 tablespoon of the oil. Mix well and allow to stand for 10 minutes.

3 Peel wide strips of the lime skin, carefully trim away the white pith and cut the rind into very fine strips. Juice the limes.

4 Heat the remaining oil in a cast iron or heavy-based pan, or on a barbecue plate, over high heat. Cook the prawns in batches until they are golden. Remove from the pan and transfer to a serving dish. Drizzle with the lime juice and season well with salt and pepper. Scatter the ginger and lime rind over the top. Serve with rice.

COOK'S FILE

Note: Freshly made curry pastes, as shown on page 101, give the best results. Leftover pastes will keep for up to 3 weeks in an airtight container in the refrigerator. If time is short, buy a ready-made paste.

Use a toothpick or tweezers to remove the veins from the prawns.

Mix the prawns with the curry paste and 1 tablespoon of the oil.

Use a sharp knife to remove the white pith and cut the rind into thin strips.

Cook the prawns in a cast iron or heavy-based pan until they are golden.

TOM YUM GOONG
(Hot and Sour Prawn Soup)

Preparation time: 25 minutes
Total cooking time: 50 minutes
Serves 4–6

500 g (1 lb) medium-sized raw prawns
1 tablespoon oil
2 litres water
2 tablespoons red curry paste
2 tablespoons tamarind concentrate
2 teaspoons turmeric
1 teaspoon chopped red chillies, optional
4 kaffir lime leaves, shredded
2 tablespoons fish sauce
2 tablespoons lime juice
2 teaspoons soft brown sugar
1/4 cup (7 g/1/4 oz) fresh coriander leaves

1 Remove the prawn heads; set aside. Peel the prawns, leaving tails intact. Using a sharp knife, slit each prawn down the back and devein. Set aside.
2 Heat the oil in a large wok or pan. Add the prawn shells and heads to the wok and cook for 10 minutes over medium-high heat, tossing frequently, until shells and heads are deep orange. Reheat the wok to very hot.
3 Gradually add 1 cup (250 ml/8 fl oz) of the water and the curry paste to the wok. Boil for 5 minutes, until reduced slightly. Add the remaining water and simmer for 20 minutes. Strain, reserving the stock. Discard heads and shells. Return the stock to the wok.
4 Add the tamarind concentrate, turmeric, chillies and lime leaves to the wok; bring to the boil and cook for 2 minutes. Add the peeled prawns to the wok and cook for 5 minutes, or until the prawns turn pink. Stir in the fish sauce, lime juice and sugar. Sprinkle with coriander leaves just before serving.

COOK'S FILE

Hint: Tamarind concentrate is available already processed, in jars, and varies in strength. It gives an acidic effect to the soup.
Note: Fresh coriander leaves, often used as a garnish, give this soup a distinctive Thai flavour.

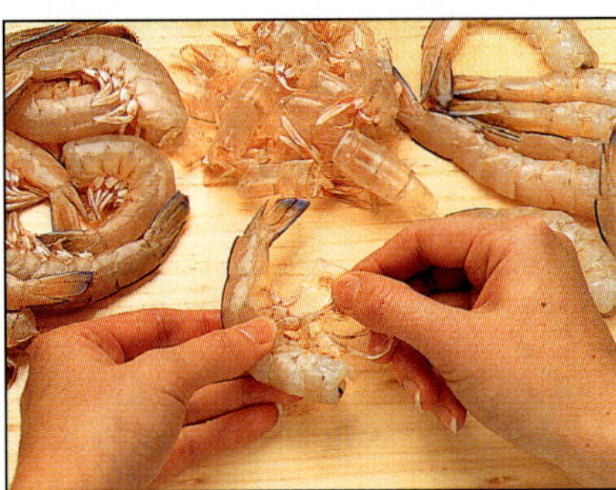

Remove the shells from the prawns, leaving the tails intact.

Fry the prawn heads and shells in the oil until they are deep orange.

Strain the stock, discard prawn heads and shells and return stock to the wok.

Add the tamarind, turmeric, chillies and shredded kaffir lime leaves to the stock.

TOM KHA GAI
(Chicken and Coconut Soup)

Preparation time: 20 minutes
Total cooking time: 20 minutes
Serves 4

5 cm (2 inch) piece fresh galangal
2 cups (500 ml/16 fl oz) coconut milk
1 cup (250 ml/8 fl oz) chicken stock
3 chicken breast fillets, cut into thin strips
1–2 teaspoons finely chopped red chillies
2 tablespoons fish sauce
1 teaspoon soft brown sugar
1/4 cup (7 g/1/4 oz) fresh coriander leaves

1 Peel the galangal and cut it into thin slices. Combine the galangal, coconut milk and stock in a medium pan. Bring to the boil and simmer, uncovered, over low heat for 10 minutes, stirring occasionally.

2 Add the chicken strips and chillies to the pan and simmer for 8 minutes.

3 Stir in the fish sauce and brown sugar. Add the coriander leaves and serve immediately, garnished with extra sprigs of coriander, if you like.

COOK'S FILE

Hint: If fresh galangal is not available, you can use 5 large slices of dried galangal instead. Prepare it by soaking the slices in a little boiling water for 10 minutes and then cutting them into small shreds. Add the soaking liquid to chicken stock to make 1 cup (250 ml/8 fl oz) and use it in the recipe.

Break the galangal so you have a piece measuring about 5 cm (2 inches).

Add the chicken strips and chillies to the simmering coconut milk mixture.

Just before serving, add the fresh coriander leaves to the pan.

PHAD THAI
(Stir-fried Rice Noodles)

Preparation time: 25 minutes
Total cooking time: 10–15 minutes
Serves 4

250 g (8 oz) dried rice sticks
2 tablespoons oil
3 cloves garlic, finely chopped
1 teaspoon chopped red chillies
150 g (4¾ oz) pork, thinly sliced
100 g (3⅓ oz) raw prawn meat, chopped
75 g (2½ oz) garlic chives, chopped
2 tablespoons fish sauce
2 tablespoons lime juice
2 teaspoons soft brown sugar
2 eggs, beaten
1 cup (90 g/3 oz) bean sprouts, scraggly ends removed
sprigs of fresh coriander
¼ cup (40 g/1⅓ oz) roasted peanuts, chopped

1 Soak the rice sticks in boiling water for 10 minutes or until they are soft. Drain and set aside. Heat the oil in a wok or large frying pan. When the oil is hot, add the garlic, chillies and pork and stir-fry for 2 minutes.

2 Add the prawn meat and stir-fry for 3 minutes. Add the garlic chives and drained rice sticks to the wok; cover and cook for another minute.

3 Add the fish sauce, lime juice, sugar and eggs to the wok; toss well with tongs or 2 wooden spoons, until the egg is set. Sprinkle with sprouts, coriander and peanuts.

COOK'S FILE

Variation: Instead of prawns and pork, use chicken and/or tofu. Add sliced carrots and bok choy.

Soak the dried rice stick noodles in boiling water until they are soft.

Add the chopped garlic chives to the wok and stir well.

Add the fish sauce, lime juice, brown sugar and beaten eggs to the wok; toss.

Grate the palm sugar until you have 3 teaspoonsful.

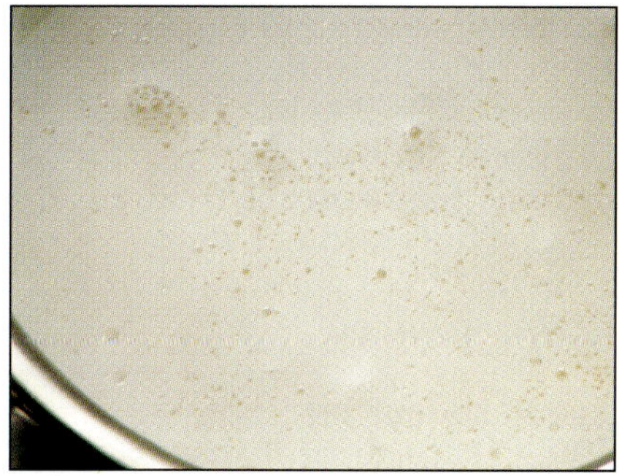

Bring the coconut milk to the boil and cook until the surface cracks.

Add the chicken strips to the wok and then stir-fry.

Season the mixture with fish sauce, lime juice and sugar.

GREEN CHICKEN CURRY

Preparation time: 25 minutes
Total cooking time: 25 minutes
Serves 4

2 cups (500 ml/16 fl oz) coconut milk
2 tablespoons oil
1 onion, chopped
2 tablespoons green curry paste
500 g (1 lb) chicken thigh fillets, cut into strips
1/4 cup (60 ml/2 fl oz) water
4 kaffir lime leaves
100 g (3 1/3 oz) snake beans, chopped
2 tablespoons fish sauce
2 tablespoons lime juice
1 teaspoon finely grated lime rind
3 teaspoons grated palm sugar or soft brown sugar
coriander leaves, to garnish

1 In a pan, bring the coconut milk to the boil and cook over high heat for about 10 minutes, until small bubbles of oil begin to crack the surface of the coconut milk.

2 Heat the oil in a wok or a heavy-based pan. Add the onion and curry paste to the wok and cook over high heat for about 1 minute, until the spices are fragrant. Add the chicken and stir-fry for 5 minutes, until the chicken is almost cooked.

3 Add the coconut milk, water, kaffir lime leaves and snake beans to the wok. Bring to the boil, stirring occasionally. Reduce the heat and simmer, uncovered, for 10 minutes, or until the chicken is tender.

4 Stir in the fish sauce, lime juice, rind and sugar. Garnish with coriander leaves. Serve with steamed rice.

COOK'S FILE

Notes: Use the recipe on page 101 to make curry paste or buy it ready-made.

- The 'cracking' of the coconut milk is a traditional technique used in Thai cookery. It separates the oils in the milk, giving the desired gloss.

MUSAMAN BEEF CURRY

Preparation time: 30 minutes
Total cooking time: 50 minutes
Serves 4

Musaman Curry Paste
1 tablespoon coriander seeds
1 tablespoon cumin seeds
seeds from 4 cardamom pods
2 teaspoons black peppercorns
1 tablespoon shrimp paste
1 teaspoon nutmeg
1/2 teaspoon ground cloves
15 dried red chillies
1/2 cup (80 g/2 2/3 oz) chopped Asian shallots
2 stems lemon grass (white part only), finely chopped
6 small cloves garlic, chopped
1 tablespoon oil

2 tablespoons oil
500 g (1 lb) topside or rump steak, cut into large cubes
1–2 tablespoons Musaman Curry Paste
2 medium onions, chopped
4 potatoes, cut into large pieces
2 1/2 cups (600 ml/20 fl oz) coconut milk
1/4 teaspoon ground cardamom
1 cinnamon stick
2 tablespoons tamarind concentrate
3 teaspoons soft brown sugar
1/2 cup (125 ml/4 fl oz) water
1/4 cup (40 g/1 1/3 oz) chopped roasted peanuts

1 To make Paste: In a small pan, dry-fry the seeds for 3 minutes. Finely grind the seeds and peppercorns in a mortar and pestle. Mix in a food processor with remaining ingredients for 20 seconds. Scrape the sides of the bowl; process in short bursts until a smooth paste forms. (Freeze unused paste in an ice cube tray, transfer to a container and freeze for up to 3 months.)
2 Heat the oil in a wok or heavy-based pan. Brown the meat in batches over high heat. Drain on paper towels.
3 Add the curry paste to the wok; stir for 1 minute. Add the onion and potato and stir until golden. Add the meat.
4 Stir in the coconut milk, cardamom, cinnamon, tamarind, sugar and water. Bring to the boil, reduce the heat and simmer, uncovered, for 20 minutes or until the meat is tender. Discard the cinnamon stick. Stir the peanuts through or sprinkle on top.

For the Musaman Curry Paste, dry-fry the seeds before grinding.

Stir-fry the meat, in batches, in a wok, until brown. Set aside on paper towels.

Add the potato and onion to the curry paste in the wok.

Stir in the coconut milk, cardamom, tamarind, sugar and water.

FRESH SPRING ROLLS

Preparation time: 30 minutes
Total cooking time: Nil
Makes 8

50 g (1⅔ oz) dried rice vermicelli
8 dried rice paper wrappers
2 hard-boiled eggs, peeled and quartered
16 fresh Thai basil leaves
½ cup (15 g/½ oz) fresh coriander leaves
½ cup (10 g/⅓ oz) fresh mint leaves
2 tablespoons chopped roasted peanuts
1 carrot, cut into short, thin strips
1 Lebanese cucumber, cut into short, thin strips
1 tablespoon grated lime rind
2 tablespoons sweet chilli sauce

Dipping Sauce
3 tablespoons hoisin sauce
1 tablespoon fish sauce
1 tablespoon cold water
2 teaspoons finely chopped chillies

1 Soak the rice vermicelli in a bowl of boiling water for 10 minutes, to soften, and then drain.
2 Dip a rice paper wrapper in a bowl of lukewarm water to soften it. Remove, drain and place on a work surface.
3 Place one of the egg quarters in the centre of the wrapper and top with 2 basil leaves, some coriander leaves, mint leaves, peanuts, a few carrot and cucumber strips, a little lime rind and a small amount of rice vermicelli. Spoon a little chilli sauce over the top.
4 Press the filling down gently, fold the bottom over, bring in the 2 sides and roll up. Lay seam-side-down on a serving plate, sprinkle with water and cover with plastic wrap. Repeat with the remaining ingredients. Rice paper wrappers must be kept moist, otherwise they will become brittle. Continue to sprinkle with cold water while rolling up, and if leaving for any length of time before serving.
5 To make Dipping Sauce: Mix all the ingredients in a bowl. Serve with Fresh Spring Rolls.

Using a sharp knife, cut the carrot and cucumber into short, thin strips.

Soften a rice paper wrapper by dipping it in a bowl of lukewarm water.

Place one of the egg quarters in the centre of the softened wrapper.

Fold the bottom over, then the two sides and roll the parcel to enclose the filling.

RED VEGETABLE CURRY

Preparation time: 25 minutes
Total cooking time: 20 minutes
Serves 4

225 g (7¼ oz) bamboo shoots or tips, drained
2 cups (500 ml/16 fl oz) coconut milk
½ cup (125 ml/4 fl oz) water
2 tablespoons red curry paste
1 medium onion, finely chopped
4 kaffir lime leaves
2 medium potatoes, roughly chopped
200 g (6½ oz) pumpkin, roughly chopped
150 g (4¾ oz) green beans, cut into short pieces
1 red capsicum, chopped
3 small zucchini, chopped
2 tablespoons chopped fresh basil leaves
2 tablespoons fish sauce
2 tablespoons lime juice
3 teaspoons soft brown sugar

1 Cut the bamboo shoots in half, discard the tough ends and set shoots aside. Combine the coconut milk, water and curry paste in a large wok or pan. Bring to the boil, stirring occasionally.

2 Add the onion and kaffir lime leaves and allow to boil for 3 minutes.

3 Add the potato and pumpkin to wok and cook over medium heat for 8 minutes, or until the pumpkin is nearly cooked. Add the beans, capsicum and zucchini and simmer for another 5 minutes. Add ½ cup of water if the curry is too thick. Add the bamboo shoots and basil. Season with fish sauce, lime juice and sugar. Serve with steamed rice.

COOK'S FILE

Note: Red curry paste recipe is on page 101. Bamboo shoot tips are available in cans and jars, in brine.

Cut the bamboo shoots in half and discard the tough ends.

Stir in the onion and kaffir lime leaves and boil for 3 minutes.

Add potato and pumpkin to the curry; simmer until pumpkin is almost cooked.

PAN-FRIED CRUSTED FISH CURRY

Preparation time: 30 minutes
+ 15 minutes soaking
Total cooking time: 10 minutes
Serves 4

4 medium dried red chillies
100 g (3 1/3 oz) Asian shallots
3 cloves garlic, chopped
2 stems lemon grass (white part only), finely sliced
4 coriander roots
2 teaspoons lime rind
1/2 teaspoon green peppercorns, roughly chopped
1/2 cup (125 ml/4 fl oz) oil
4 medium boneless fish fillets (approximately 750 g/1 1/2 lb)
1/2 cup (125 ml/4 fl oz) thin coconut milk
1 tablespoon fish sauce
4 kaffir lime leaves, finely shredded
2 tablespoons lime juice

1 Soak the red chillies in a bowl of boiling water for 15 minutes, or until softened. Drain and chop roughly.

2 Process the chillies, shallots, garlic, lemon grass, coriander roots, lime rind and peppercorns in a food processor, until paste is smooth. Add 1 tablespoon of the oil to help the processing and regularly scrape down sides of the bowl with a rubber spatula. Spread the paste lightly over one side of the fish fillets.

3 Heat the remaining oil in a heavy-based or cast iron pan. Cook the fish in a single layer, or batches if necessary, for 2–3 minutes on each side, until just cooked, turning over carefully with 2 egg slices so the fish doesn't break.

4 Mix the coconut milk, fish sauce, lime leaves and juice in a small jug. Pour over the fish, reduce the heat and simmer for 3 minutes. Remove the fish from the pan, using an egg slice.

To prevent skin irritation, wear rubber gloves when cutting up the chillies.

Process the mixture in a food processor until a smooth paste forms.

Use two egg slices to carefully turn the fish over, without breaking it.

MEE GROB
(Crispy Fried Noodles)

Preparation time: 30 minutes + drying
Total cooking time: 20 minutes
Serves 4

100 g (3$^1/_3$ oz) dried rice vermicelli
2 cups (500 ml/16 fl oz) oil
100 g (3$^1/_3$ oz) fried tofu, cut into matchsticks
2 cloves garlic, finely chopped
4 cm (1$^1/_2$ inch) piece of fresh ginger, grated
150 g (4$^3/_4$ oz) chicken or pork mince, or combination of both
100 g (3$^1/_3$ oz) raw prawn meat, finely chopped
1 tablespoon white vinegar
2 tablespoons fish sauce
2 tablespoons soft brown sugar
2 tablespoons chilli sauce
1 teaspoon chopped red chillies
2 small knobs pickled garlic, chopped
40 g (1$^1/_3$ oz) fresh garlic chives, chopped
1 cup (30 g/1 oz) fresh coriander leaves

1 Soak the rice vermicelli in a bowl of boiling water for 1 minute. Drain and allow to dry for 20 minutes.
2 Heat the oil in a wok or deep pan, add the tofu in two batches and cook for 1 minute or until crisp and golden. Drain on paper towels.
3 Add the completely dry vermicelli to the wok in several batches, cooking for 10 seconds or until puffed and crisp. Remove from the oil immediately, to prevent the vermicelli absorbing too much oil. Drain on paper towels and allow to cool.
4 Drain all but 1 tablespoon of the oil from the wok. Reheat the wok over high heat and add the garlic, ginger, mince and prawn meat. Stir-fry for 3 minutes. Add the vinegar, fish sauce, sugar, chilli sauce and chillies; stir until boiling. Just before serving, add the noodles and tofu to the wok and toss thoroughly. Quickly toss the pickled garlic, garlic chives and coriander leaves through. Serve immediately or it will become soggy.

Drain the vermicelli in a colander and set aside until completely dry.

Cook the tofu, in two batches, until crisp and golden. Drain on paper towels.

When the vermicelli is completely dry, fry in batches for 10 seconds, or until crisp.

Add the vinegar, fish sauce, sugar, chilli sauce and chillies to the wok.

CHICKEN SALAD ON A BED OF WATERCRESS

Preparation time: 40 minutes
Total cooking time: 10–15 minutes
Serves 4

3 small chicken breast fillets (about 350 g/$11\frac{1}{4}$ oz)
1 medium Lebanese cucumber
$\frac{1}{2}$ red capsicum
150 g ($4\frac{3}{4}$ oz) watercress
$\frac{1}{2}$ cup (10 g/$\frac{1}{3}$ oz) small fresh mint leaves
2 tablespoons finely shredded fresh mint leaves, to garnish
2 chillies, finely sliced, and 2 tablespoons crisp-fried onion, to garnish

Dressing
3 tablespoons lime juice
2 tablespoons coconut milk
1 tablespoon fish sauce
1 tablespoon sweet chilli sauce

1 Line a bamboo steaming basket with baking paper and steam the chicken, covered, over a wok or pan of simmering water, for 10 minutes or until the chicken is cooked through. Remove from the heat and set aside to cool. Thinly slice the cucumber and cut the slices in half. Slice the capsicum into thin strips.

2 While the chicken is cooling, pick over the watercress and separate the sprigs from the tough stems. Arrange the watercress and whole mint leaves on a serving plate. Using your fingers, tear the chicken into long fine shreds. Gently toss the shredded chicken, cucumber and capsicum in a bowl. Arrange over the watercress bed. Drizzle the dressing over the salad and sprinkle with the shredded fresh mint, sliced chillies and crisp-fried onion.

3 To make Dressing: Thoroughly whisk the lime juice, coconut milk, fish sauce and sweet chilli sauce.

COOK'S FILE

Note: Crisp-fried, or sometimes deep-fried, onions are available in packets or small jars from Asian food speciality stores.

Line a bamboo steamer with baking paper and cook the chicken.

Separate the sprigs from the tough stems of the watercress.

When the chicken is cooked, tear it into shreds, using your fingers.

CRISP FRIED FISH WITH TAMARIND SAUCE

Preparation time: 20 minutes
+ 10 minutes standing
Total cooking time: 25 minutes
Serves 4

2 medium-sized red fish (total weight about 1 kg/ 2 lb), cleaned and scaled
2 tablespoons red curry paste
1½ cups (375 ml/12 fl oz) oil, for deep-frying
3 cm (1¼ inch) piece of fresh ginger, grated
2 red capsicums, very finely sliced
6 spring onions, finely chopped
3 tablespoons tamarind concentrate
1½ cups (375 ml/12 fl oz) coconut milk
2 tablespoons fish sauce
1 tablespoon lime juice

1 Wash the fish and pat dry with paper towels. Using a sharp knife, score a criss-cross pattern on both sides of the fish. Spread the curry paste over the fish (your fingertips are best for this job). Set aside for 10 minutes.

2 Meanwhile, using 1 tablespoon of the oil, heat a frying pan over high heat and stir-fry the ginger, capsicum and spring onion for 5 minutes. Add the tamarind and coconut milk. Bring the sauce to the boil and cook for 5 minutes, or until thickened slightly. Add the fish sauce and lime juice, stir to combine, remove from the heat and set aside.

3 Heat the remaining oil in a wok and when hot, carefully deep-fry the fish, one at a time, for about 3 minutes each side. Use two wooden spoons to move the fish around, to cook the head and tail. Be careful not the break the tail and fins. Drain on paper towels and transfer to a warm oven while cooking the other fish. Arrange on a serving platter. Transfer the sauce to a small serving bowl for spooning over the top. (You can serve the sauce at room temperature or reheat just before serving.)

Carve a shallow criss-cross pattern on both sides of the fish.

Cook the sauce, stirring occasionally, for 5 minutes, or until it thickens slightly.

Use two wooden spoons to gently move the fish around to cook the head and tail.

生

KOREA

POTATO NOODLES WITH VEGETABLES

Preparation time: 30 minutes + soaking
Total cooking time: 25 minutes
Serves 4

300 g (9⅔ oz) dried potato starch noodles
30 g (1 oz) dried cloud-ear fungus
¼ cup (60 ml/2 fl oz) sesame oil
2 tablespoons vegetable oil
3 cloves garlic, finely chopped
4 cm (1½ inch) piece of fresh ginger, grated
2 spring onions, finely chopped
2 carrots, cut into 4 cm (1½ inch) matchsticks
2 spring onions, extra, cut into 4 cm (1½ inch) pieces
500 g (1 lb) baby bok choy or 250 g (8 oz) English spinach, roughly chopped
¼ cup (60 ml/2 fl oz) shoshoyu (Japanese soy sauce)
2 tablespoons mirin
1 teaspoon sugar
2 tablespoons sesame seed and seaweed sprinkle

1 Cook the dried potato noodles in a large pan of boiling water for about 5 minutes or until the noodles are translucent. Drain and then rinse thoroughly under cold running water until the noodles are cold. (Thoroughly rinsing the noodles will remove any excess starch.) Use kitchen scissors to roughly chop the noodles into lengths of about 15 cm (6 inches), to make the noodles easier to eat with chopsticks.

2 Pour boiling water over the fungus and soak for 10 minutes. Drain thoroughly and chop roughly. Heat 1 tablespoon of the sesame oil with the vegetable oil in a large, heavy-based pan or wok. Add the garlic, ginger and spring onion to the pan and cook for 3 minutes over medium heat, stirring regularly. Add the carrot sticks and stir-fry for 1 minute.

3 Add the cooled noodles, extra spring onion, baby bok choy or spinach, remaining sesame oil, shoshoyu, mirin and sugar. Toss well to coat the noodles with the sauce. Cover and cook over low heat for 2 minutes.

4 Add the drained fungus, cover the pan and cook for another 2 minutes. Sprinkle with the sesame seed and seaweed sprinkle. Serve immediately.

COOK'S FILE

Hints: Potato starch noodles are sometimes called Korean vermicelli.
- Cloud-ear fungus is a delicately-flavoured dried mushroom — when re-hydrated in hot water it triples in size.
- Japanese soy sauce is lighter and sweeter than Chinese soy sauce.
- All the ingredients mentioned above are available from Asian food speciality stores.

Make the noodles easier to eat by roughly chopping them with scissors.

Add the noodles, spring onion, bok choy, sesame oil, shoshoyu, mirin and sugar.

BARBECUED BEEF

Preparation time: 20 minutes
+ 30 minutes freezing
+ 2 hours marinating
Total cooking time: 15 minutes
Serves 4–6

500 g (1 lb) scotch fillet or sirloin steak
$\frac{1}{4}$ cup (40 g/1$\frac{1}{3}$ oz) sesame seeds
$\frac{1}{2}$ cup (125 ml/4 fl oz) shoshoyu (Japanese soy sauce)
2 cloves garlic, finely chopped
3 spring onions, finely chopped
1 tablespoon sesame oil
1 tablespoon oil

1 Freeze the steak for 30 minutes to make it easy to slice thinly. Dry-fry the sesame seeds over low heat for 3–4 minutes, shaking the pan gently until the seeds are golden. Remove from the pan, allow to cool and then grind in a food processor or with a mortar and pestle.

2 Slice the steak into thin strips, cutting across the grain. Combine the meat, shoshoyu, garlic, spring onion and half the crushed seeds in a bowl and toss until the meat is well coated with the sauce. Cover and marinate in the refrigerator for 2 hours.

3 Combine the oils and brush some onto a cast iron grill pan, heavy-based frying pan or barbecue plate. Heat to very hot and cook the meat in batches, searing each side for about 1 minute (don't overcook or the steak will be chewy). Oil and reheat the grill between batches. Serve steak sprinkled with the remaining crushed seeds and with pickled cabbage (Kim Chi). Shown garnished with Asian Shallot bulbs.

Cut across the grain of the meat when slicing it into thin slices.

Combine the meat with soy sauce, garlic, spring onion and half the sesame seeds.

Take care not to overcook the meat when searing it on both sides.

SPARERIBS WITH SESAME SEEDS

Preparation time: 30 minutes
Total cooking time: 1 hour 10 minutes
Serves 4–6

1 kg (2 lb) pork spareribs, cut into 3 cm ($1^1/_4$ inch) pieces
1 tablespoon sesame seeds
2 tablespoons oil
2 spring onions, finely chopped
4 cm ($1^1/_2$ inch) piece of fresh ginger, grated
3 cloves garlic, finely chopped
2 tablespoons caster sugar
2 tablespoons rice wine
1 tablespoon shoshoyu
2 teaspoons sesame oil
$1^1/_4$ cups (315 ml/10 fl oz) hot water
2 teaspoons cornflour

1 Trim the pork of excess fat. Dry-fry the sesame seeds over low heat for 3–4 minutes, shaking the pan gently, until the seeds are golden. Remove, allow to cool and then grind in a food processor or with a mortar and pestle.

2 Heat the oil in a heavy-based frying pan. Brown the spareribs over high heat, turning regularly, until dark golden. Drain any excess oil from the pan. Add half the sesame seeds with the spring onion, ginger, garlic, sugar, rice wine, shoshoyu, sesame oil and water. Cover and simmer for 45–50 minutes, stirring occasionally.

3 Combine the cornflour with a little cold water and mix to a smooth paste. Add to the pan, stirring constantly, until the mixture boils and thickens. Sprinkle with the remaining crushed sesame seeds. Serve with steamed rice and pickled cabbage (Kim Chi).

COOK'S FILE

Note: If preferred, ask your butcher to cut the ribs into smaller pieces, so they can be held with chopsticks.

Dry-fry the sesame seeds over low heat until they are golden brown.

Turn the spareribs regularly until they are dark golden.

Add the sauce to the pan and stir slowly to combine with the spareribs.

KIM CHI
(Pickled Cabbage)

Preparation time: 10 minutes
+ 9 days standing
Total cooking time: Nil
Makes approximately 3 cups

1 large Chinese cabbage
1/2 cup (160 g/5 1/4 oz) rock salt
1/2 teaspoon cayenne pepper
5 cm (2 inch) piece of fresh ginger, grated
3 teaspoons to 3 tablespoons chopped chillies (see Note)
5 spring onions, chopped
2 cloves garlic, finely chopped
1 tablespoon caster sugar
2 1/2 cups (600 ml/20 fl oz) water

1 Cut the cabbage in half, then into large bite-sized pieces. Place a layer of cabbage in a large bowl and sprinkle with a little salt. Continue with layers of cabbage and salt, finishing with salt.
2 Cover with a dinner plate that will fit as snugly as possible on top of the cabbage. Weigh down the plate with cans or a small brick and place the bowl in the refrigerator for 5 days.
3 Remove weights and plate, pour off any liquid. Rinse cabbage well under cold running water. Squeeze out excess water and combine the cabbage with cayenne pepper, ginger, chillies, spring onion, garlic and sugar. Mix well before spooning into a large, sterilized jar. Pour the water over the top and seal with a tight-fitting lid. Refrigerate for 3–4 days before using.

COOK'S FILE

Note: Kim Chi is an accompaniment to Korean meals. Use quantity of chillies between the suggested range, according to your taste. It may seem a lot, but 3 tablespoons is the authentic quantity.

Layer cabbage pieces in a bowl, sprinkling with salt between each layer and on top.

Fit a plate snugly on top of the cabbage and weigh the plate down with cans.

Squeeze any excess water from the cabbage, using your hands.

SPLIT PEA AND RICE PANCAKES WITH VEGETABLES

Preparation time: 40 minutes
Total cooking time: 50 minutes
Makes 15–20 pancakes

1 cup (220 g/7 oz) dried green split peas
1/2 cup (110 g/3 2/3 oz) short-grain rice
1/2 cup (60 g/2 oz) plain flour
2 eggs, beaten
1 cup (250 ml/8 fl oz) water
1/2 green and 1/2 red capsicum
6 spring onions
1 carrot
3 cm (1 1/4 inch) piece of fresh ginger, finely grated
2 cloves garlic, finely chopped
2 teaspoons shoshoyu
2 tablespoons vegetable oil
1 tablespoon sesame oil
dipping sauce (see page 100) or bottled sweet chilli sauce

1 Wash the split peas and rice in a colander under cold running water, until water runs clear. Transfer to a large pan, cover with cold water and bring to the boil. Cook for 25 minutes, adding more water if necessary, or until the peas are very soft. Drain. Allow to cool and then purée in a food processor. Add the flour, eggs and most of the water and process in short bursts until a smooth batter forms, adding sufficient water to achieve a thick pouring consistency. (You may need more than 1 cup.)

2 Remove the membrane and seeds from both the red and green capsicum. Trim the spring onions. Cut the vegetables into fine matchsticks about 5 cm (2 inches) long. Pour the batter into a bowl and stir in the vegetables, ginger, garlic and shoshoyu.

3 Combine the vegetable and sesame oils in a bowl. Brush a heavy-based pan with some combined oil and heat the pan to moderately hot. Cook the pancakes, pouring in 2 tablespoons of batter for each, for 3–5 minutes. When the base is cooked, run an egg slice around the edge, turn over and cook for 2 minutes. Cover for 30 seconds to ensure the pancake is cooked. Transfer to a plate and keep warm in a very slow oven while cooking the rest. Brush the pan with oil before cooking each batch. Serve with dipping sauces.

When the peas and rice are cool, process in a food processor until smooth.

Using a sharp knife, cut the vegetables into very fine matchstick lengths.

Very gently turn the pancakes and cook them for another 2 minutes.

CRISP POTATO PANCAKES

Preparation time: 25 minutes
Total cooking time: 30 minutes
Makes approximately 18

Dipping Sauce
2 teaspoons sesame seeds
2 cloves garlic, finely chopped
2 spring onions, very finely sliced
1/4 cup (60 ml/2 fl oz) shoshoyu (Japanese soy sauce)
1 tablespoon white wine
1 tablespoon sesame oil
2 teaspoons caster sugar
1 teaspoon chopped red chillies

500 g (1 lb) potatoes
1 large onion, very finely chopped
2 eggs, beaten
2 tablespoons cornflour
1/4 cup (60 ml/2 fl oz) oil

1 To make Dipping Sauce: Dry-fry the sesame seeds over low heat for 3–4 minutes, shaking the pan gently, until the seeds are golden. Remove, allow to cool and then grind in a food processor or with a mortar and pestle. Combine with the garlic, spring onion, shoshoyu, wine, sesame oil, sugar and chillies. Mix well and then transfer to a serving bowl.

2 Peel the potatoes and grate them on the coarse side of a grater. Place in a large bowl with the onion, eggs and cornflour; season with salt and pepper, to taste. Stir thoroughly to make sure the cornflour is mixed through.

3 Heat the oil in a large heavy-based frying pan (an electric frying pan is suitable). Using 2 spoons, drop 1 heaped tablespoon of mixture onto the hot surface and spread out gently with the back of the spoon so the pancake is about 6 cm (2 1/2 inches) in diameter. Cook for 2–3 minutes or until golden. Cook 4–5 pancakes, or as many as you can fit in the pan at one time.

4 Turn over and cook for another 2 minutes. Do not have the pan too hot or the pancakes will burn and not cook through. Keep the pancakes warm while cooking the remainder. Serve with the sauce as a snack or with rice and pickled cabbage (Kim Chi) as part of a meal.

Grate the peeled potatoes on the coarse side of a grater.

Drop rounded tablespoonsful of the mixture into the hot oil.

Spread the pancakes to about 6 cm (2 1/2 inches) in diameter.

Turn the pancakes over with an egg slice and brown the other side.

FRIED NOODLES

Preparation time: 30 minutes
Total cooking time: 25 minutes
Serves 4

1/4 cup (40 g/1 1/3 oz) sesame seeds
2 tablespoons oil
2 teaspoons sesame oil
4 spring onions, chopped
2 cloves garlic, finely chopped
150 g (4 3/4 oz) raw prawn meat
2 teaspoons finely chopped red chillies
150 g (4 3/4 oz) fresh firm tofu, cut into small cubes
100 g (3 1/3 oz) button mushrooms, thinly sliced
1 red capsicum, cut into thin strips
2 tablespoons water
2 tablespoons shoshoyu
2 teaspoons sugar
300 g (9 2/3 oz) packet Hokkien noodles

1 Dry-fry the sesame seeds over low heat for 3–4 minutes, shaking the pan gently, until the seeds are golden. Remove, allow to cool and then grind in a food processor or mortar and pestle.

2 Combine the oils in a small bowl. Heat half the oil mixture in a wok or a large heavy-based frying pan, over medium-high heat. Add the spring onion, garlic and prawn meat and stir-fry for 1 minute. Add the chillies, stir for another minute; remove mixture from the pan and set aside. Add the tofu to the pan, tossing occasionally until lightly golden; remove from the pan and set aside. Add the remaining oil to the pan, add the vegetables and stir-fry for 3 minutes or until just crisp.

3 Add the water, shoshoyu, sugar and noodles to the pan. Toss gently to separate and coat the noodles in liquid. Cover and steam for 5 minutes; toss well. Add the prawn mixture and tofu and toss for 3 minutes over medium heat. Sprinkle with the crushed sesame seeds and serve.

Use a wooden spoon to stir the onion, garlic and prawn meat.

Stir-fry the tofu, tossing occasionally until lightly golden. Remove and set aside.

Add the water, soy sauce and noodles to the pan and toss gently.

JAPAN

SUSHI

Preparation time: 45 minutes
Total cooking time: 8–10 minutes
Makes approximately 30

1 cup (220 g/7 oz) short-grain white rice
2 cups (500 ml/16 fl oz) water
1 tablespoon caster sugar
1 teaspoon salt
2 tablespoons rice vinegar
125 g (4 oz) smoked salmon, trout or fresh sashimi tuna
1 small Lebanese cucumber, peeled
1/2 small avocado, optional
4 sheets nori
wasabi, to taste
3 tablespoons pickled ginger or vegetables
shoshoyu, for dipping

1 Wash the rice in cold water until the water runs clear and then drain thoroughly. Place the rice and water in a medium pan. Bring to the boil, reduce heat and simmer, uncovered, for 4–5 minutes or until all the water is absorbed. Cover and reduce the heat to very low and cook for another 4–5 minutes. Remove the pan from the heat and cool, covered, for 10 minutes.

2 Add the combined caster sugar, salt and rice vinegar to the rice, tossing with a wooden spoon until well combined. Set aside.

3 Cut the salmon into thin strips. Cut the cucumber and avocado into matchsticks about 5 cm (2 inches) long. Place a sheet of nori on a sushi mat or a piece of greaseproof paper, on a flat surface with the longest sides at the top and bottom. Spread a quarter of the rice over about half of the nori, leaving a 2 cm (3/4 inch) border around the remaining 3 sides. Spread a very small amount of wasabi down the centre of the rice. Arrange a quarter of the pieces of fish, cucumber, avocado and ginger or vegetables along the top of the wasabi.

4 Using the mat or paper as a guide, roll the nori up firmly from the bottom, enclosing the rice around the ingredients. Press the nori edges together to seal the roll. Using a very sharp or electric knife, cut the roll into 2.5 cm (1 inch) rounds. Repeat with remaining ingredients. Serve with shoshoyu and extra wasabi for dipping.

COOK'S FILE

Storage time: Sushi rolls can be made up to 4 hours in advance and kept, covered, in the refrigerator. Slice into pieces just before serving.

Notes: Fresh sashimi tuna is available from good fishmongers — make sure the fish is extremely fresh.

- Sushi mats are available in Asian speciality stores and make the rolling of sushi much easier.
- Shoshoyu is Japanese soy sauce, sweeter and lighter than Chinese soy.

Spread one quarter of the rice along about one half of each nori sheet.

Starting at the bottom, roll the nori up to enclose the rice and filling.

PRAWN AND VEGETABLE TEMPURA

Preparation time: 40 minutes
Total cooking time: 15 minutes
Serves 4

20 large raw prawns
plain or tempura flour, for coating
1¾ cups (215 g/6¾ oz) tempura flour
1¾ cups (440 ml/14 fl oz) iced water
2 egg yolks
oil, for deep-frying
1 large zucchini, cut into strips
1 red capsicum, cut into strips
1 onion, cut into rings
shoshoyu, for dipping

1 Shell and devein the prawns, leaving the tails intact. Make four incisions in the underside of each prawn and straighten the prawns out flat.

2 Coat the prawns lightly with flour, leaving the tail uncoated. In a bowl, gently mix the tempura flour, water and egg yolks and use at once (the batter will be lumpy — don't overmix).

3 Heat the oil in a deep pan or wok. Dip each prawn into the batter, still leaving the tail uncoated. Fry quickly in the hot oil. When lightly golden, remove from the pan and drain well on paper towels. Repeat with the vegetable strips, about 2–3 pieces at a time. Add strips of fresh ginger to the shoshoyu if you like.

COOK'S FILE

Note: Tempura flour is available from speciality Asian shops, and makes the lightest tempura batter. Plain flour can be used but the batter will be slightly heavier.

Carefully cut four incisions into the underside of each prawn.

Lightly mix the batter, using chopsticks or a wooden spoon (it will be lumpy).

Hold the prawn by the tail and dip it in the batter, leaving the tail uncoated.

FRIED PORK AND NOODLES

Preparation time: 30 minutes
Total cooking time: 15 minutes
Serves 4

1 tablespoon vegetable oil
150 g (4¾ oz) pork loin, cut into small strips
5 spring onions, cut into short lengths
1 carrot, cut into thin strips
200 g (6½ oz) Chinese cabbage, shredded
500 g (1 lb) Hokkien noodles, gently pulled apart to separate
2 tablespoons water
2 tablespoons shoshoyu
1 tablespoon Worcestershire sauce
1 tablespoon mirin
2 teaspoons caster sugar
1 cup (90 g/3 oz) bean sprouts, scraggly ends removed
1 sheet toasted nori, cut into finè, thin shreds

1 Heat the vegetable oil in a large deep pan or wok over medium heat. Stir-fry the pork, spring onion and carrot for 1–2 minutes, or until the pork just changes colour. Take care not to overcook or the pork will toughen and the vegetables will become limp.

2 Add the cabbage, noodles, water, shoshoyu, Worcestershire sauce, mirin and sugar. Cover and cook for 1 minute.

3 Add the bean sprouts to the pan and use two large metal spoons or spatulas to coat the vegetables and noodles in the sauce. Serve immediately, sprinkled with the shredded nori.

Finely shred the Chinese cabbage with a large, sharp knife.

Use your fingers to remove the scraggly ends from the bean sprouts.

Stir-fry the pork, spring onion and carrot until the pork just changes colour.

SASHIMI
(Raw Sliced Fish)

Preparation time: 30 minutes
Total cooking time: Nil
Serves 4

500 g (1 lb) very fresh seafood such as tuna, salmon, kingfish, ocean trout, snapper, whiting bream or jewfish
1 carrot, peeled, to garnish
1 daikon, peeled, to garnish
shoshoyu (Japanese soy sauce), for serving
wasabi, for serving

1 Clean the fish and then use a very sharp, flat-bladed knife to remove any skin. Chill the fish in the freezer until it is sufficiently firm to be cut into thin, evenly-sized slices, about 5 mm (1/4 inch) wide — cut with an even motion, taking care not to saw.
2 Use a zester to scrape carrot or daikon into long thin strips or cut them into julienne strips. Use to garnish the sashimi.
3 Arrange the prepared sashimi pieces and garnishes attractively on a flat platter and serve immediately with a bowl of shoshoyu and the wasabi for mixing, to taste, for dipping.

COOK'S FILE

Note: It is crucial that the fish used for making Sashimi is of the highest quality. You can use either one kind of fish or a mixture of different types of fish. Frozen seafood should not be used. Sashimi should be prepared just before serving. Different garnishes of your choice can be used.

Use a very sharp, flat-bladed knife to remove the skin from the fish.

Cut the trout and piece of tuna into even slices about 5 mm (1/4 inch) thick.

For garnishing, use a zester to scrape long, thin strips of carrot and daikon.

YAKITORI
(Chicken on Skewers)

Preparation time: 20 minutes
+ soaking
Total cooking time: 10 minutes
Makes 25 skewers

1 kg (2 lb) chicken thigh fillets
1/2 cup (125 ml/4 fl oz) sake
3/4 cup (185 ml/6 fl oz) shoshoyu (Japanese soy sauce)
1/2 cup (125 ml/4 fl oz) mirin
2 tablespoons sugar
10 spring onions, cut diagonally into 2 cm (3/4 inch) pieces

1 Soak 25 wooden skewers in water for about 20 minutes in water. Drain and set them aside.

2 Cut the chicken thigh fillets into bite-sized pieces. Combine the sake, shoshoyu, mirin and sugar in a small pan. Bring the mixture to the boil and then set aside.

3 Thread the chicken pieces onto the wooden skewers, alternately with the spring onion pieces. Place the skewers on a foil-lined tray and cook them under a preheated grill, turning and brushing frequently with the sauce, for 7–8 minutes, or until the chicken is cooked through. Serve immediately, garnished with a few spring onion pieces, or sprigs of fresh herbs.

COOK'S FILE

Note: In Japan, Yakitori is usually served as a snack with beer. The addition of steamed rice and your favourite vegetables turn these delicious kebabs into a satisfying meal.

Use a sharp knife to cut the chicken into bite-sized pieces.

Thread the chicken pieces and spring onion alternately onto the skewers.

Frequently brush the chicken with the sauce as it cooks.

CHICKEN DOMBURI

Preparation time: 35 minutes
Total cooking time: 30 minutes
Serves 4

2 cups (440 g/14 oz) short-grain rice
2½ cups (600 ml/20 fl oz) water
2 tablespoons oil
2 small chicken breasts (about 250 g/8 oz), cut into thin strips
2 medium onions, thinly sliced
4 tablespoons water, extra
4 tablespoons shoshoyu
2 tablespoons mirin
1 teaspoon dashi granules
5 eggs, lightly beaten
2 sheets nori
2 spring onions, sliced

1 Wash the rice in a colander under cold running water until the water runs clear. Transfer the rice to a heavy-based pan, add the water and bring to the boil over high heat. Cover the pan with a tight-fitting lid and reduce the heat to as low as possible (otherwise the rice in the bottom of the pan will burn) and cook for 15 minutes. Turn the heat to very high, for 15–20 seconds, remove the pan from the heat and set aside for 12 minutes, without lifting the lid (don't allow the steam to escape).

2 Heat the oil in a frying pan over high heat; stir-fry the chicken until tender. Remove the chicken from the pan; set aside. Reheat the pan, add the onion and cook, stirring occasionally, 3 minutes, or until beginning to soften. Add the extra water, shoshoyu, mirin and dashi granules. Stir to dissolve the dashi and bring stock to the boil. Cook for 3 minutes or until onion is tender.

3 Return the chicken to the pan and pour in the eggs, stirring gently to just break up. Cover and simmer over very low heat for 2–3 minutes or until the eggs are just set. Remove the pan from heat. To make the nori crisp, hold it over low heat, moving it back and forward for about 15 seconds, and then crumble it into small pieces.

4 Transfer the rice to a serving dish, carefully spoon over the chicken and egg mixture and sprinkle with nori. Garnish with the spring onion.

COOK'S FILE

Notes: Domburi is an earthenware dish and food served in the dish is also known as domburi.

• The Japanese technique of cooking rice uses a 'burst' of heat before the standing time. A rice cooker can be used to cook the rice if preferred.

Wash the rice in a colander under cold running water.

Cook the onion for about 3 minutes, until it begins to soften.

Add the eggs to the pan and stir gently to break them up.

TOFU MISO SOUP

Preparation time: 15 minutes
Total cooking time: 7 minutes
Serves 4

250 g (8 oz) firm tofu
1 spring onion
4 cups (1 litre) water
$\frac{1}{2}$ cup (80 g/$2\frac{2}{3}$ oz) dashi granules
100 g ($3\frac{1}{3}$ oz) miso
1 tablespoon mirin

1 Use a sharp knife to cut the tofu into 1 cm ($\frac{1}{2}$ inch) cubes. Slice the spring onion diagonally into short lengths. Set the tofu and spring onion aside.

2 Using a wooden spoon, combine the water and dashi in a small pan, and then bring the mixture to the boil.

3 Combine the miso and mirin in a small bowl and then add to the boiling liquid in the pan. Reduce the heat to medium and stir the miso, taking care not to let the mixture boil once the miso is dissolved (overheating will result in the loss of miso flavour). Add the tofu cubes to the hot stock and heat, without boiling, over medium heat, for 5 minutes. Serve in individual soup bowls, garnished with the slices of spring onion.

COOK'S FILE

Note: Soup is an essential part of Japanese cuisine. Miso soup is a popular, simple, clear soup with a subtle flavour. There are many variations and they all taste good. Use deep soup bowls if possible, so that the soup stays hot.

Use a sharp knife to carefully cut the tofu into small cubes.

Combine the water with the dashi in a small pan, stirring with a wooden spoon.

Mix the miso and the mirin in a small bowl until well combined.

UDON NOODLE SOUP WITH PORK AND LEEKS

Preparation time: 20 minutes
Total cooking time: 16 minutes
Serves 4

400 g ($12\frac{2}{3}$ oz) dried udon noodles
1 litre water
3 teaspoons dashi granules
2 medium leeks (white and pale green parts), well washed and cut into very thin slices
200 g ($6\frac{1}{2}$ oz) pork loin, cut into thin strips
$\frac{1}{2}$ cup (125 ml/4 fl oz) shoshoyu (Japanese soy sauce)
2 tablespoons mirin
4 spring onions, very finely chopped
shichimi togarashi

1 Cook the noodles in a large pan of rapidly boiling water for 5 minutes, or until tender. Drain and then cover to keep warm.

2 Combine the water and dashi in a large pan, bring to the boil, add the leeks, reduce the heat and simmer for 5 minutes. Add the pork, shoshoyu, mirin and spring onion; simmer for 2 minutes or until the pork is cooked.

3 Divide the noodles among four serving bowls, ladle the soup over the top, garnish with spring onion and sprinkle with shichimi togarashi.

COOK'S FILE

Note: Shichimi togarashi is a finely ground seasoning sprinkled on many Japanese dishes. It is available from Japanese speciality stores. If you can't find it, use your favourite pepper.

Gently lower the noodles into a large pan of rapidly boiling water.

Simmer the leeks for 5 minutes until they have softened.

Add the pork, shoshoyu, mirin and spring onion to the pan.

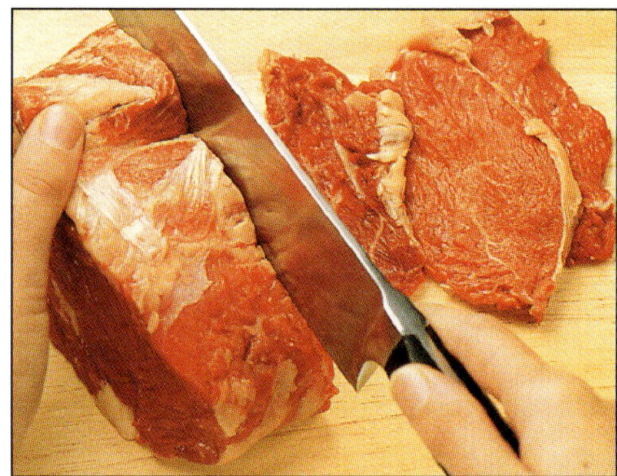

Use a large, sharp knife to cut the steak into very thin slices.

Trim the ends from the eggplants and cut them into long, thin slices.

Carefully cut the hard stems from the fresh shiitake mushrooms.

When one side of the meat is seared, turn over and quickly sear the other side.

TEPPAN YAKI
(Grilled Steak and Vegetables)

Preparation time: 50 minutes
Total cooking time: 25 minutes
Serves 4

350 g (11¼ oz) scotch fillet, partially frozen
4 small slender eggplants
100 g (3⅓ oz) fresh shiitake mushrooms
100 g (3⅓ oz) baby green beans
6 baby yellow or green squash
1 red or green capsicum
6 spring onions, outside layer removed
210 g (6¾ oz) can bamboo shoots, drained
¼ cup (60 ml/2 fl oz) light vegetable oil
Soy and Ginger Dipping Sauce (see page 100), for serving

1 Slice the steak into very thin pieces — this is easier if the steak is partially frozen. Place the slices in a single layer on a large serving platter, season with plenty of salt and freshly ground pepper and set aside while the vegetables are being prepared.

2 Trim the ends from the eggplants and cut them into long, very thin slices. Trim the mushrooms; top and tail the beans. If the beans are longer than about 7 cm (2¾ inches), halve them. Quarter or halve the squash, or leave whole, depending on their size.

3 Cut the capsicum into thin strips and slice the spring onion into lengths of about 7 cm (2¾ inches), discarding the tops. Trim the bamboo shoot slices to a similar size. Arrange all the vegetables attractively, in separate bundles, on a serving plate.

4 When guests are seated, heat an electric grill, griddle or frying pan until very hot and lightly brush it with oil. Quickly fry about a quarter of the meat, searing on both sides, and push it to the edge of the pan. Quickly stir-fry about a quarter of the vegetables in the grill or pan, adding more oil as needed. Serve a small portion of meat and vegetables to each guest. The food should be dipped in sauce just before being eaten. Repeat the process with the remaining meat and vegetables, cooking in batches as extra helpings are required. Serve with steamed rice.

VIETNAM

BEEF PHO

Preparation time: 45 minutes
Total cooking time: 4 hours 10 minutes
Serves 4

1 kg (2 lb) beef shin bones
350 g (11 1/4 oz) gravy beef
5 cm (2 inch) piece of fresh ginger, thinly sliced
1 teaspoon salt
2.5 litres water
6 black peppercorns
1 cinnamon stick
4 cloves
6 coriander seeds
2 tablespoons fish sauce
400 g (12 2/3 oz) fresh thick rice noodles
red chillies, sliced; bean sprouts; fresh purple basil leaves; spring onions, chopped; thin lime wedges, to garnish
150 g (4 3/4 oz) rump steak, thinly sliced
3 spring onions, finely chopped
1 medium onion, very thinly sliced
1/4 cup (7 g/1/4 oz) fresh coriander leaves, optional
chilli sauce and hoisin sauce, optional

1 Place the bones, beef, ginger, salt and water in a large pan. Bring to the boil, reduce heat to low and simmer for 3 1/2 hours. Skim off any scum that forms on the surface. Add the peppercorns, cinnamon, cloves, coriander and fish sauce; cook for another 40 minutes. Remove the gravy beef, set aside to cool. Drain the stock, reserving the liquid and discarding the bones and spices; return the stock to the pan. When the beef is cool enough to touch (otherwise, use rubber gloves) cut it, across the grain, into very fine slices. Set aside.

2 Close to serving time, plunge the noodles into a pan of boiling water and cook for about 10 seconds only, otherwise they will soften and fall apart. Drain the noodles well and divide among large soup bowls.

3 Arrange the garnishes on a platter in the centre of the table. Bring the beef stock to a rapid boil. Place some slices of the cooked meat on top of each bowl of noodles, as well as a few slices of the raw steak. Ladle the boiling stock over the top and sprinkle with the spring onion, onion slices and coriander, if using; serve. Each guest chooses the desired garnishes. Sauces such as chilli or hoisin can be available for adding to the dish.

COOK'S FILE

Note: The success of this beef soup with salad depends on the full-flavoured stock, for which there is no quick substitute. Even though it takes a long time to cook, it is well worth the effort. The stock can be made in advance and frozen, making it easy to put the dish together when required.

Remove the purple basil leaves from the stems. Prepare the other garnishes.

Strain the stock through a colander, reserving all the liquid.

SPRING ROLLS

Preparation time: 50 minutes + soaking
Total cooking time: 25 minutes
Makes approximately 20

50 g ($1\frac{2}{3}$ oz) dried mung bean vermicelli (cellophane noodles)
8 pieces dried cloud-ear fungus
20–25 rice paper wrappers (to allow for damaged ones)
4 spring onions, finely chopped
1 medium carrot, cut into thin matchsticks
170 g ($5\frac{1}{2}$ oz) can good-quality crab meat, well drained
150 g ($4\frac{3}{4}$ oz) pork mince
$\frac{1}{4}$ teaspoon each salt and pepper
1 teaspoon sugar
1 egg, beaten
oil, for deep-frying
20 butter or soft-leaf lettuce leaves
1 cup (20 g/$\frac{2}{3}$ oz) fresh mint leaves
1 cup (90 g/3 oz) bean sprouts, scraggly ends removed
dipping sauce (see page 100) or bottled sweet chilli sauce

1 Soak the dried noodles and fungus in 2 separate bowls, in enough hot water to cover, for 15 minutes. Drain well and use scissors to roughly chop the noodles into shorter lengths and the fungus into fine slivers. Transfer to a large bowl.
2 Using a pastry brush, brush both sides of each rice paper wrapper with water. Leave on the bench for about 2 minutes, until the wrappers become soft and pliable. Stack on top of each other; sprinkle lightly with water to keep moist or they will stick together and dry out. Work carefully as the wrappers can tear easily when softened.
3 To the noodles and fungus, add the spring onion, carrot, crab meat, pork mince, salt, pepper and sugar. Mix very well to combine. Place one softened wrapper on the bench, spread about 1 tablespoon of the filling along the bottom third of the wrapper, leaving enough space at the sides to fold the wrapper over. Using your fingertips, push out any air pockets on the wrapper. Fold in the sides towards each other and firmly roll the wrapper up. Lightly brush the seam with the egg and place the rolls seam-side-

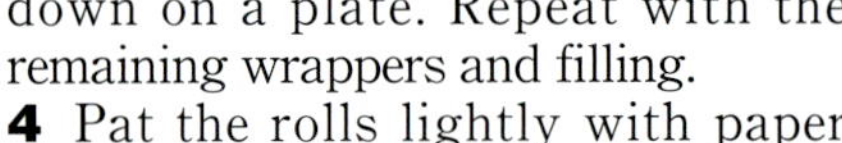

down on a plate. Repeat with the remaining wrappers and filling.
4 Pat the rolls lightly with paper towels to remove any excess water (or the oil will spit when the rolls are frying). Heat the oil in a deep pan and, when very hot, fry the rolls 2–3 at a time until golden, tossing them gently in the oil so they brown evenly. Drain on paper towels and repeat with remaining rolls. To serve, place a spring roll in each lettuce leaf, top with a few mint leaves and bean sprouts, roll up and eat with a dipping sauce.

Cover the dried noodles and fungus with boiling water and soak for 15 minutes.

Brush both sides of rice paper wrappers liberally with water to make them pliable.

Add the spring onion, carrot, crab meat, pork, salt, pepper and sugar to the bowl.

CARAMELIZED PRAWNS

Preparation time: 25 minutes
Total cooking time: 15 minutes
Serves 4

500 g (1 lb) medium raw prawns
6 spring onions
4 tablespoons sugar
1 tablespoon oil
3 cloves garlic, finely chopped
1 tablespoon fish sauce
1 tablespoon lime juice
1 tablespoon soft brown sugar
1/2 teaspoon salt
1/4 red capsicum, cut into fine strips

1 Remove the prawn heads but leave the tails, shells and legs intact. Using a fine needle, devein the prawns. Rinse the prawns under running water and pat dry with paper towels.

2 Finely chop half the spring onions. Cut the rest into 4 cm (1 1/2 inch) pieces and finely shred into thin strips.

3 To make a caramel sauce, combine the sugar with 3 tablespoons of water in a small pan. Stir over low heat, without boiling, until sugar has dissolved. Bring to the boil, reduce heat and simmer gently for 5 minutes, or until the syrup turns dark golden. Take care not to burn it. Remove the pan from the heat and add 4 tablespoons of water — it will spit and sizzle, and the caramel will form hard lumps — return to the heat until the lumps become liquid again.

4 Heat the oil in heavy-based frying pan over medium heat. Add the garlic, chopped spring onion and prawns. Cook for 3 minutes, tossing the prawns until they turn pink. Drizzle the caramel sauce and fish sauce over the top; cook for 1 minute. Add the lime juice, sugar, salt and remaining spring onion; toss well. Serve immediately, garnished with capsicum.

COOK'S FILE

Note: If the prawn shells are tender, they can be eaten. Supply finger bowls and napkins so people can peel them if they prefer.

After adding water to the sauce, hard lumps will form in the bottom.

Toss the unpeeled prawns in the pan until the prawns turn pink.

Add the lime juice, sugar, salt and remaining spring onion to the pan.

CHICKEN CURRY

Preparation time: 30 minutes
Total cooking time: 1 hour
Serves 4

1.5 kg (3 lb) chicken pieces, such as thighs, drumsticks and wings
2 tablespoons oil
4 cloves garlic, finely chopped
5 cm (2 inch) piece of fresh ginger, finely chopped
2 stems lemon grass (white part only), finely chopped
2 teaspoons dried chilli flakes
2 tablespoons curry powder
2 brown onions, chopped
2 teaspoons sugar
1 teaspoon salt
1 1/2 cups (375 ml/12 fl oz) coconut milk
1/2 cup (125 ml/4 fl oz) water
fresh garlic chives, cut into long strips; fresh coriander leaves and roasted peanuts, to garnish

1 Using a large heavy knife or cleaver, chop each piece of chicken into two, chopping straight through the bone. Pat the chicken pieces dry with paper towels.

2 Heat the oil in a large deep frying pan. Add the garlic, ginger, lemon grass, chilli and curry powder and stir constantly over medium heat for 3 minutes. Add the chicken pieces, onion, sugar and salt; toss gently. Cover, cook for 8 minutes, or until the onion has softened and then toss well to coat the pieces evenly with the curry mixture. Cover again and cook for 15 minutes over low heat — the chicken will gently braise, producing its own liquid.

3 Add the coconut milk and water to the pan and bring to the boil, stirring occasionally. Reduce the heat and simmer, uncovered, for 30 minutes or until the chicken is very tender. Serve garnished with the chives, coriander and peanuts.

COOK'S FILE

Note: Asian curry powders are available from speciality shops. There are different mixtures available for meat, chicken or fish.

Chop each piece of chicken into two pieces, or ask your butcher to do it.

Toss the chicken pieces through the curry mixture, using two wooden spoons.

Add the coconut milk and water to the curry and stir well.

GREEN PAWPAW, CHICKEN AND FRESH HERB SALAD

Preparation time: 30 minutes
Total cooking time: 10 minutes
Serves 4

2 medium chicken breast fillets (about 350 g/11¼ oz)
1 large green pawpaw
1 cup (20 g/⅔ oz) fresh Vietnamese mint leaves
½ cup (15 g/½ oz) fresh coriander leaves
2 red chillies, seeded and finely sliced
2 tablespoons fish sauce
1 tablespoon rice wine vinegar
1 tablespoon lime juice
2 teaspoons sugar
2 tablespoons chopped roasted peanuts

1 Place the chicken in a frying pan with enough water to just cover. Simmer over gentle heat for 10 minutes or until the chicken is cooked. Don't let the water boil — it should just gently simmer, to poach the chicken. Remove the chicken from the liquid and allow to cool completely. Finely slice the chicken.

2 Using a potato peeler, peel the pawpaw and then cut the flesh into thin strips. Mix gently in a bowl with the mint and coriander, sliced chilli, fish sauce, vinegar, lime juice and sugar.

3 Arrange the pawpaw mixture on a serving plate and pile the chicken on top. Scatter the peanuts over the top and serve immediately.

COOK'S FILE

Note: Green pawpaw is underripe pawpaw, used for tartness and texture.

Gently simmer the chicken breast fillets until they are cooked through.

Use a sharp knife to cut the cooled chicken into thin pieces.

Cut the peeled pawpaw into long, thin strips, using a very sharp knife.

STIR-FRIED CHICKEN WITH LEMON GRASS, GINGER AND CHILLI

Preparation time: 30 minutes
Total cooking time: 15–20 minutes
Serves 4

2 tablespoons oil
2 brown onions, roughly chopped
4 cloves garlic, finely chopped
5 cm (2 inch) piece of fresh ginger, finely grated
3 stems lemon grass (white part only), very finely sliced
2–3 teaspoons chopped green chillies
500 g (1 lb) chicken thigh fillets, thinly sliced
2 teaspoons sugar
1 tablespoon fish sauce
green chillies, extra, sliced; fresh coriander and Vietnamese mint leaves, to garnish

1 Heat the oil in a heavy-based frying pan or wok and add the onion, garlic, ginger, lemon grass and chillies. Stir for 3–5 minutes over medium heat, until the mixture is lightly golden. Take care not to burn the mixture or it will be bitter.

2 Increase the heat, add the chicken slices and toss well. Sprinkle the sugar over the chicken and cook for approximately 5 minutes, tossing regularly until just cooked.

3 Add the fish sauce, cook for another 2 minutes and serve garnished with sliced green chillies, fresh coriander and mint. Serve with steamed rice.

COOK'S FILE

Hints: Be sure to cook this stir-fry quickly in a very hot wok, or the chicken will stew in its own juices.

- Lemon grass imparts a delightful lemony flavour to food. Make sure the stems you buy are not dried out.

Use a sharp knife to finely slice the white part of the lemon grass.

Sprinkle the sugar over the chicken mixture and cook for about 5 minutes.

Just before serving, add the fish sauce and cook for another 2 minutes.

Soak the dried Chinese mushroom pieces in hot water for 20 minutes.

Use a cleaver or heavy knife to chop the duck into small pieces.

Brown the duck pieces over medium heat, turning regularly so they don't burn.

Add the soy sauce, wine, sugar, orange peel and mushrooms to the pan.

BRAISED DUCK WITH MUSHROOMS

Preparation time: 30 minutes + soaking
Total cooking time: 1 hour 10 minutes
Serves 6

1 cup (15 g/½ oz) dried sliced Chinese mushroom pieces
1.5 kg (3 lb) duck
2 teaspoons oil
2 tablespoons soy sauce
2 tablespoons rice wine
2 teaspoons sugar
2 wide strips fresh orange peel, plus extra to garnish
125 g (4 oz) watercress

1 Soak the mushrooms in hot water for 20 minutes. Drain well.

2 Using a heavy knife or cleaver, chop the duck into small pieces, cutting through the bone. Arrange on a rack in a baking dish and pour boiling water over them to plump up the skin and keep them succulent. Drain, pat dry with paper towels and set aside.

3 Brush the base of a heavy-based frying pan with the oil and heat over medium heat. Brown the duck pieces, turning regularly, in 2 or 3 batches depending on the size of the pan, browning each batch for 8 minutes. In between each batch, wipe out the pan with crumpled paper towels to remove excess oil. (The darker the browning at this stage, the better the colour when finished.)

4 Wipe the pan with paper towels again and return the duck pieces to the pan. Add the soy sauce, rice wine, sugar, orange peel and mushrooms to pan. Bring the mixture to the boil, reduce the heat until simmering, cover and cook gently for 35 minutes or until the duck is tender. Using a soup spoon, carefully skim off any surface oil. Season with salt and pepper, to taste, and allow to stand for 10 minutes, covered, before serving. Remove and discard the orange peel. Pick off small sprigs of the watercress and arrange on a large serving plate. Place the duck segments on the plate — try not to place the duck on the watercress as it will become soggy. Spoon a little of the sauce over the duck just before serving. Garnish with strips of orange rind.

PORK AND LETTUCE PARCELS

Preparation time: 40 minutes + cooling
Total cooking time: 45 minutes
Serves 4–6

500 g (1 lb) pork loin
5 cm (2 inch) piece of fresh ginger, thinly sliced
1 tablespoon fish sauce
20 spring onions
2 butter or soft-leaf lettuces
1 long cucumber, thinly sliced
1/4 cup (5 g/1/4 oz) fresh mint leaves
1/4 cup (7 g/1/4 oz) fresh coriander leaves
2 green chillies, seeded and very finely sliced, optional
2 teaspoons sugar
Lemon and Garlic Dipping Sauce (see page 100), for serving

1 Place the pork, ginger, fish sauce and enough cold water to cover in a pan. Cover and simmer for about 45 minutes, or until the pork is tender. Remove the pork and allow to cool for 15 minutes. Discard the liquid.

2 While the pork is cooking, trim both ends from all the spring onions, so that you have long thin even-sized stems. Bring a large pot of water to the boil and, using tongs, blanch the spring onions, 2 or 3 at a time, for 1 minute, or until softened. Remove from the hot water and place in a bowl of ice-cold water. Drain and lay flat and straight on a tray, to be used later.

3 Cut the pork into thin slices and finely shred each slice. If the pork is too hot to touch, wear clean rubber gloves. Spread out one lettuce leaf at a time, place about 1 tablespoon of the shredded pork in the centre of the leaf. Top with a few slices of cucumber, a few fresh mint and coriander leaves, a little chilli, and a light sprinkling of sugar. Fold a section of the lettuce over the filling, bring in the sides to meet each other and carefully roll up the parcel. Tie one of the spring onions around the parcel, trim off the excess or tie into a bow. Repeat with the remaining ingredients. Arrange the parcels on a serving platter and serve with Lemon and Garlic Dipping Sauce.

COOK'S FILE

Hint: If the lettuce leaves have a firm section in the centre, at the base of the leaf, trim this away, or rolling into a neat parcel will be difficult.

Use a sharp knife to trim both ends from all the spring onions.

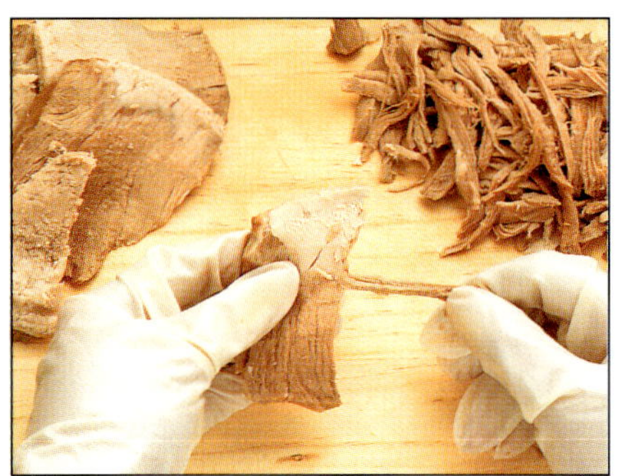

Shred the cooked pork into thin pieces. Use rubber gloves if the pork is too hot.

Bring in the two sides of the lettuce to meet and then roll up the parcel.

CHICKEN WITH PINEAPPLE AND CASHEWS

Preparation time: 35 minutes
Total cooking time: 25 minutes
Serves 4

1/2 cup (80 g/2 2/3 oz) raw cashews
2 tablespoon oil
4 cloves garlic, finely chopped
1 large onion, cut in large chunks
2 teaspoons chopped red chillies
350g (11 1/4 oz) chicken thigh fillets, chopped
1/2 red capsicum, chopped
1/2 green capsicum, chopped
2 tablespoons oyster sauce
1 tablespoon fish sauce
1 teaspoon sugar
2 cups (320 g/10 1/4 oz) chopped fresh pineapple
3 spring onions, chopped
2 tablespoons shredded coconut, toasted

1 Roast the cashews on an oven tray for about 15 minutes in a moderate 180°C (350°F/Gas 4) oven, until deep golden; allow to cool.

2 Heat the oil in a wok or a large, deep frying pan and stir-fry the garlic, onion and chillies over medium heat for 2 minutes; remove from the wok. Increase the heat to high and stir-fry the chicken and capsicum, in 2 batches, tossing until the chicken is light brown. The heat must be very high so the chicken will be succulent.

3 Return the onion mixture to the wok, add the oyster sauce, fish sauce, sugar and pineapple and toss for 2 minutes. Toss the cashews through. Arrange on a serving plate and scatter the spring onion and coconut over the top. Serve immediately with rice, garnished with fresh coriander leaves.

Roast the cashews on an oven tray for 15 minutes or until golden.

Stir-fry the chicken and capsicum until the chicken is light brown.

Return the onion mixture to the wok and stir through with a wooden spoon.

CHILLI PRAWN AND SNAKE BEAN STIR-FRY

Preparation time: 25 minutes
Total cooking time: 10–15 minutes
Serves 4

2 tablespoons oil
2 medium onions, very finely sliced
5 cloves garlic, finely chopped
2 stems lemon grass (white part only), very finely sliced
3 red chillies, seeded and very finely sliced
250 g (8 oz) snake beans, topped and tailed and cut into short pieces
300 g (9 2/3 oz) medium raw prawns, peeled and deveined
2 teaspoons sugar
1 tablespoon fish sauce
1 tablespoon rice wine vinegar
garlic chives, chopped, to garnish

1 Heat the oil in a large heavy-based wok. Add the onion, garlic, lemon grass and chillies to the wok and stir-fry over medium-high heat for 4 minutes or until soft and golden.
2 Add the beans to the wok and stir-fry for 2–3 minutes or until bright green. Add the prawns and sugar to the wok and toss gently for 3 minutes.
3 Season with the fish sauce and rice wine vinegar, toss well and serve, sprinkled with garlic chives.

COOK'S FILE

Note: Snake beans are very long, dark green beans, about 30 cm (12 inches) long, with pointed tips. They are sold in bunches at speciality fruit and vegetable and Asian food stores. If they are not available, green beans may be used.

Top and tail the snake beans and then cut them into short pieces.

Stir-fry the onion, garlic, lemon grass and chillies in the wok.

Add the chopped snake beans to the wok and stir-fry until they are bright green.

SWEET BRAISED PUMPKIN

Preparation time: 20 minutes
Total cooking time: 30 minutes
Serves 4

750 g (1 1/2 lb) pumpkin
1 1/2 tablespoons oil
3 cloves garlic, finely chopped
4 cm (1 1/2 inch) piece of fresh ginger, grated
6 Asian shallots, chopped
1 tablespoon soft brown sugar
1/2 cup (125 ml/4 fl oz) chicken stock
2 tablespoons fish sauce
1 tablespoon lime juice

1 Peel the pumpkin and cut into large chunks. Heat the oil in a heavy-based frying pan, add the garlic, ginger and shallots and cook for 3 minutes over medium heat, stirring regularly.
2 Add the pumpkin pieces, sprinkle with sugar. Cook for 8–10 minutes, turning the pieces regularly until the pumpkin is golden and just tender.
3 Add the chicken stock and fish sauce, bring to the boil and cook, turning the pumpkin over regularly, until all the liquid has evaporated. Sprinkle with lime juice, season to taste with salt and pepper; serve. Delicious with a curry or plenty of steamed rice.

COOK'S FILE

Note: The sweeter pumpkins, such as butternut or Japanese are delicious and produce an appealing soft texture.

Use a large knife or cleaver to cut the peeled pumpkin into large chunks.

Add the pumpkin to the garlic mixture and cook, turning regularly, until golden.

Add the stock and fish sauce to pan and continue cooking until liquid evaporates.

Chilli Prawn and Green Bean Stir-fry (top) and Sweet Braised Pumpkin

EGGPLANT SLICES IN BLACK BEAN SAUCE

Preparation time: 20 minutes
Total cooking time: 35 minutes
Serves 4

500 g (1 lb) medium eggplant
1/3 cup (80 ml/2 3/4 fl oz) oil
4 cloves garlic, finely chopped
4 cm (1 1/2 inch) piece of fresh ginger, grated
2 medium onions, finely chopped
1/3 cup (80 ml/2 3/4 fl oz) chicken stock
2 teaspoons salted black beans, rinsed well, roughly chopped
2 tablespoons oyster sauce
1 tablespoon soy sauce
2 teaspoons fish sauce
4 spring onions, sliced into long diagonal strips

1 Slice the eggplant into long slices and lightly brush each side with oil.
2 Heat a frying pan over medium heat and cook 4–5 slices of eggplant at a time until golden on both sides. Don't hurry this process as slow cooking of the eggplant slices allows the natural sugars to caramelize and produces a wonderful flavour. If the eggplant begins to burn, reduce the heat and sprinkle with a little water.
3 When all the eggplant is browned, remove from pan and set aside. Increase the heat to medium-high, add any remaining oil and add the garlic, ginger, onion and 1 tablespoon of chicken stock. Cover and cook for 3 minutes. Add the remaining stock, black beans, oyster, soy and fish sauces. Bring to the boil and cook for 2 minutes. Return the eggplant to the pan and simmer for 2 minutes or until heated through. Scatter the spring onion over the top.

COOK'S FILE

Note: Salted black beans are available from Asian food stores. After opening, they'll keep indefinitely if refrigerated. Rinse very well before using, or they'll be extremely salty.

Rinse the black beans well under cold running water.

Use a long, sharp knife to cut the eggplant into long slices.

Cook the eggplant slices over medium heat until golden on both sides.

WARM BEEF AND WATERCRESS SALAD

Preparation time: 25 minutes
+ 30 minutes standing
Total cooking time: 10 minutes
Serves 4

350 g (11¼ oz) fillet steak, partially frozen
1 tablespoon green peppercorns, roughly chopped
4 cloves garlic, finely crushed
3 stems lemon grass (white part only), very finely sliced
3 tablespoons oil
¼ teaspoon each salt and freshly ground black pepper
250 g (8 oz) watercress
125 g (4 oz) cherry tomatoes, halved
4 spring onions, chopped
2 tablespoons lime juice

1 Cut the steak into thin slices and combine in a bowl with the peppercorns, garlic, lemon grass, 2 tablespoons oil, salt and pepper. Mix well, cover and refrigerate 30 minutes.

2 Meanwhile, remove the watercress sprigs from the tough stems and break into small pieces. Wash and drain well; arrange on a platter. Arrange the tomatoes over the top.

3 Heat the remaining oil in a wok or heavy-based frying pan until very hot and lightly smoking. Add the beef mixture and quickly stir-fry until the meat is just cooked. Toss the spring onion through. Remove from the pan, pile up in the centre of the watercress and sprinkle lime juice all over the top. Serve immediately.

COOK'S FILE

Note: The steak is easier to slice thinly when partially frozen.

Cut the partially frozen steak into very thin slices.

Pull the watercress sprigs off the tough stems and break into small pieces.

Quickly stir-fry the beef mixture until the meat is just cooked.

FRIED RICE NOODLE PANCAKE WITH GARLIC BEEF

Preparation time: 20 minutes + 30 minutes marinating
Total cooking time: 30 minutes
Serves 4

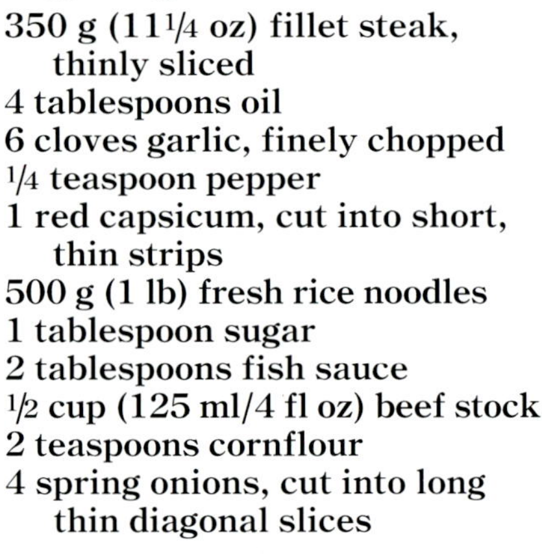

350 g (11¼ oz) fillet steak, thinly sliced
4 tablespoons oil
6 cloves garlic, finely chopped
¼ teaspoon pepper
1 red capsicum, cut into short, thin strips
500 g (1 lb) fresh rice noodles
1 tablespoon sugar
2 tablespoons fish sauce
½ cup (125 ml/4 fl oz) beef stock
2 teaspoons cornflour
4 spring onions, cut into long thin diagonal slices

1 Combine the steak, half the oil, the garlic, pepper and capsicum. Cover and refrigerate for 30 minutes.

2 Gently separate the noodles. Add the remaining oil to a heavy-based medium-sized pan and swirl well to coat. Heat the pan over medium heat. Add the noodles, pressing them down firmly, with a spatula, into a flat large pancake the size of the pan. Cook for 10–15 minutes, pressing down occasionally, until the base is very crisp and golden. Do not disturb or lift the noodles as they need to form a solid base. Run a spatula underneath the pancake to loosen the base, and, using 2 egg slices, turn the pancake over to cook the other side. Be patient, because, if the pancake is moved before it sets, it will break up. Transfer to a plate, cover and keep warm.

3 Heat a heavy-based pan or wok to very hot. Toss the beef mixture over high heat, in 2 batches, sprinkling with sugar and fish sauce, for 2–3 minutes. Stir the stock and cornflour in a bowl until a smooth paste forms. Add to the meat; toss for 1 minute. Don't overcook the meat or it will become tough.

4 To serve, place the pancake on a large serving plate, cut into serving wedges and top with the beef and capsicum, piling it up in the centre. Garnish with the spring onion and serve immediately.

Use your fingers to gently separate the fresh rice noodles.

Press the noodles down firmly, using a spatula, to form a large pancake.

Use two egg slices to transfer the pancake to a plate.

Add the stock and cornflour mixture to the pan and toss for 1 minute.

BARBECUED FISH WITH ONIONS AND GINGER

Preparation time: 25 minutes
+ 20 minutes marinating
Total cooking time: 25 minutes
Serves 4–6

750g (1½ lb) small firm, white-fleshed fish, cleaned and scaled
2 teaspoons green peppercorns, finely crushed
2 teaspoons chopped red chillies
3 teaspoons fish sauce
2 teaspoons oil
1 tablespoon oil, extra
2 medium onions, finely sliced
4 cm (1½ inch) piece of fresh ginger, peeled and cut into very thin slices
3 cloves garlic, cut into very thin slivers
2 teaspoons sugar
4 spring onions, cut into 4 cm (1½ inch) pieces, then finely shredded
Lemon and Garlic Dipping Sauce (see page 100), for serving

1 Wash the fish inside and out and pat dry with paper towels. Cut 2 diagonal slashes into the thickest part of the fish on both sides. In a food processor or mortar and pestle, grind the peppercorns, chillies and fish sauce to a paste and brush lightly over the fish. Allow to stand for 20 minutes.

2 Heat a grillplate or flatplate until very hot and lightly brush with oil. Cook the fish for 8 minutes on each side, or until the flesh flakes easily when tested. If grilling the fish, make sure it is not too close to the heat or it will burn.

3 While the fish is cooking, heat the extra oil in a pan and stir the onion over medium heat, until golden. Add the ginger, garlic and sugar; cook for 3 minutes. Place the fish on a serving plate, top with the onion mixture and sprinkle with spring onion. Serve immediately with Lemon and Garlic Dipping Sauce and wedges of lemon or lime.

Cut 2 diagonal slashes into the thickest part of the fish, using a sharp knife.

Lightly brush the chilli mixture over the surface of the fish.

Cook the finely sliced onion over medium heat, stirring until golden.

BEAN VERMICELLI AND CRAB MEAT STIR-FRY

Preparation time: 20 minutes
+ 20 minutes soaking
Total cooking time: 10–15 minutes
Serves 4

200 g (6½ oz) dried mung bean vermicelli (cellophane noodles)
2 tablespoons oil
10 Asian shallots, very finely sliced
3 cloves garlic, finely chopped
2 stems lemon grass (white part only), very finely sliced
1 red capsicum, cut into thin 4 cm (1½ inch) matchsticks
170 g (5½ oz) can crab meat, well-drained
2 tablespoons fish sauce
2 tablespoons lime juice
2 teaspoons sugar
3 spring onions, cut into very fine diagonal slivers

1 Soak the noodles in boiling water for 20 minutes or until softened. Drain and snip the noodles several times with scissors, to shorten the lengths for easy eating.

2 Heat the oil in a wok or heavy-based pan, over high heat. Add the Asian shallots, garlic and lemon grass and stir-fry for 2–3 minutes. Add the capsicum and cook for 30 seconds, tossing well. Add the noodles and toss. Cover and steam for 1 minute, or until the noodles are heated through.

3 Add the crab meat, fish sauce, lime juice and sugar; toss well, using two wooden spoons. Season with salt and pepper, sprinkle with spring onion and serve.

COOK'S FILE

Hint: Fresh crab meat is delicious in this dish, if available. Some fish markets sell fresh crab meat in airtight refrigerated packs.

Finely slice the white section of the fresh lemon grass, using a sharp knife.

Snip the noodles several times with scissors, to make them easier to eat.

Add the noodles to the wok, toss and steam, covered, for 1 minute.

FRIED RICE

Preparation time: 40 minutes
Total cooking time: 15–20 minutes
Serves 4

3 cups (555 g/1 lb 1¾ oz) cold cooked rice
3 eggs
¼ teaspoon salt
½ cup (125 ml/4 fl oz) oil
1 large onion, finely chopped
6 spring onions, chopped
4 cloves garlic, finely chopped
5 cm (2 inch) piece of fresh ginger, finely grated
2 small red chillies, seeded and finely chopped
250 g (8 oz) pork loin, finely chopped
125 g (4 oz) Chinese dried sausages, thinly sliced
100 g (3⅓ oz) green beans, chopped
100 g (3⅓ oz) carrots, diced
½ large red capsicum, diced
2 teaspoons sugar
3 tablespoons fish sauce
2 tablespoons soy sauce
fresh coriander leaves, to garnish

1 If the rice grains are sticking together, sprinkle with 2 tablespoons of water and use a fork to separate the grains.

2 Whisk the eggs and salt in a bowl until frothy. Heat 1 tablespoon of the oil in a wok and swirl it around to coat the sides. Pour in the egg and cook gently over medium heat, stirring regularly for 2–3 minutes, or until the egg is just cooked. Remove from the wok and set aside.

3 Wipe the wok with a paper towel and return to the heat. Add 1 more tablespoon of oil and, when hot, cook the onion, spring onion, garlic, ginger and chillies for 7 minutes, stirring regularly, or until the onion is golden and softened; remove from the wok. Add another tablespoon of oil and, when hot, stir-fry the pork and sausage for 3–4 minutes or until cooked; remove from wok and set aside.

4 Add the remaining oil to the wok and swirl to coat the sides. Add the beans, carrots and capsicum and stir-fry for 1 minute over high heat. Add the rice to the wok and toss well to coat with the vegetables and oil; stir-fry for 2 minutes. Add the onion and meat mixtures, sugar, fish and soy sauces and salt, to taste, and toss well for 30 seconds or until heated through. Add the scrambled egg and toss lightly. Serve sprinkled with coriander leaves.

COOK'S FILE

Note: Chinese spicy pork sausages (lup chiang) are available fresh or in airtight packets from Asian food stores. Freeze for up to 3 months.

Use a fork to separate the grains of the cooked rice, if they are sticking together.

Cook the eggs over medium heat, stirring until just cooked.

Stir-fry the pork and sausage in the wok, until cooked.

MALAYSIA

BARBECUED SEAFOOD

Preparation time: 30 minutes
+ 15 minutes marinating
Total cooking time: 10 minutes
Serves 6

1 medium onion, grated
4 cloves garlic, chopped
5 cm (2 inch) piece of fresh ginger, grated
3 stems lemon grass (white part only), chopped
2 teaspoons ground or grated fresh turmeric
1 teaspoon shrimp paste
1/3 cup (80 ml/2 3/4 fl oz) vegetable oil
1/4 teaspoon salt
4 medium calamari tubes
2 thick white boneless fish fillets
8 raw king prawns
2 limes, cut into wedges
banana leaves, for serving

1 Combine the onion, garlic, ginger, lemon grass, turmeric, shrimp paste, oil and salt in a small food processor. Process in short bursts until the mixture forms a paste.

2 Cut the calamari in half lengthways and lay it on the bench with the soft inside facing up. Score a very fine honeycomb pattern into the soft side, taking care not to cut all the way through, and then cut into large pieces. Wash all the seafood under cold running water and pat dry with paper towels. Brush the seafood lightly with the spice paste. Place the seafood on a tray, cover and refrigerate for 15 minutes.

3 Lightly oil a barbecue hotplate and heat. When the plate is hot, arrange the fish fillets and prawns side-by-side on the plate. Cook for about 3 minutes on each side, turning them once only, or until the fish flesh is just firm and the prawns turn bright pink to orange. Add the calamari pieces and cook for about 2 minutes or until the flesh turns white and rolls up — take care not to overcook the seafood.

4 Arrange the seafood on a platter lined with the banana leaves, add the lime wedges and serve immediately, garnished with strips of lime rind and some fresh mint, if you like. Steamed or boiled rice can be served with the seafood.

COOK'S FILE

Notes: If serving as part of a dinner party, supply finger bowls for each guest to clean their hands after peeling the prawns.

• Banana leaves are available from speciality fruit and vegetable shops. Alternatively, make friends with someone who has a banana tree.

• Seafood can be marinated longer to allow the flavours to develop more.

Variation: Any seafood can be used. Octopus, mussels, scallops and oysters would all be suitable.

Process in short bursts until the mixture forms a paste.

Score a fine honeycomb pattern into the soft side of the calamari.

FRIED RICE NOODLES

Preparation time: 30 minutes
Total cooking time: 15 minutes
Serves 4

2 Chinese dried pork sausages
2 tablespoons oil
2 cloves garlic, finely chopped
1 medium onion, finely chopped
3 red chillies, seeded and chopped
250 g (8 oz) Chinese barbecued pork, finely chopped
200 g (6 1/2 oz) raw prawn meat
500 g (1 lb) fresh thick rice noodles, gently separated
150g (4 3/4 oz) garlic chives, cut into 3 cm (1 1/4 inch) pieces
2 tablespoons kecap manis
3 eggs, lightly beaten
1 tablespoon rice vinegar
100 g (3 1/3 oz) bean sprouts, scraggly ends removed

1 Diagonally slice the dried pork sausages into paper-thin slices. Heat the oil in a large heavy-based wok or large deep frying pan. Fry the sausage, tossing regularly until golden and very crisp. Using a slotted spoon, remove from wok; drain on paper towels.

2 Reheat the oil in the wok, add the garlic, onion, chillies and pork; stir-fry for 2 minutes. Add the prawn meat and toss constantly, until prawns change colour. Add noodles, chives and kecap manis; toss. Cook for 1 minute or until the noodles begin to soften. Pour the combined eggs and vinegar over the top of the mixture and toss for 1 minute. Be careful not to overcook the noodles, or let the egg-coated noodles burn on the base of the pan.

3 Add the bean sprouts to the mixture and toss. Arrange on a large serving platter, scatter the drained pork sausages over the top and toss a little to mix a few slices among the noodles. Serve immediately, garnished with a few extra chives.

COOK'S FILE

Note: Chinese pork sausages (lup chiang) must be cooked before eating.

Chop the Chinese barbecued pork into very small pieces, using a sharp knife.

Remove the crisp Chinese sausage slices from the wok and drain on paper towels.

Pour the combined eggs and vinegar over the top of the mixture and toss.

COUNTRY CHICKEN KAPITAN

Preparation time: 35 minutes
Total cooking time: 35 minutes
Serves 4–6

30 g (1 oz) small dried prawns
4 tablespoons oil
4–8 red chillies, seeded and finely chopped
4 cloves garlic, finely chopped
3 stems lemon grass (white part only), finely chopped
2 teaspoons turmeric
10 candlenuts
2 large onions, chopped
1/4 teaspoon salt
500 g (1 lb) chicken thigh fillets, cut into bite-sized pieces
1 cup (250 ml/8 fl oz) coconut milk
1 cup (250 ml/8 fl oz) water
1/2 cup (125 ml/4 fl oz) coconut cream
2 tablespoons lime juice

1 Dry-fry the prawns, over low heat for 3 minutes, shaking the pan regularly. The prawns are ready when they turn dark orange and have a strong aroma. Pound the prawns in a mortar and pestle until finely ground, or process in a small food processor. (This ground prawn meat is called prawn floss.) Set the prawn floss aside.

2 Process half the oil with the chillies, garlic, lemon grass, turmeric and candlenuts in a food processor, in short bursts, until very finely chopped, regularly scraping down the sides of the bowl with a rubber spatula.

3 Add the remaining oil to a large, deep frying pan or heavy-based wok and cook the onion and the salt over low heat, stirring regularly, for 8 minutes, or until golden. Take care not to let the onion burn. Add the spice mixture and nearly all the prawn floss, setting a little aside to use as garnish. Stir for 5 minutes. If the mixture begins to stick to the bottom of the pan, add 2 tablespoons of the coconut milk to the mixture. It is important to cook the mixture thoroughly to develop the flavours.

4 Add the chicken to the pan and stir well. Cook for 5 minutes or until the chicken begins to brown. Stir in the coconut milk and water and bring to the boil. Reduce the heat and simmer for 7 minutes or until chicken is cooked and sauce is thick. Add the coconut cream and bring the mixture back to the boil, stirring constantly. Add the lime juice and serve immediately, sprinkled lightly with the reserved prawn floss. Serve with steamed rice.

Pound the dry-fried prawns in a mortar and pestle until finely ground.

Process the chilli mixture in shorts bursts, regularly scraping the sides of the bowl.

Stir-fry the onion and spice mixture for 5 minutes, taking care not to let it stick.

LAKSA LEMAK
(Rice Noodles and Seafood in Spicy Soup)

Preparation time: 1 hour + soaking
Total cooking time: 1 hour
Serves 4

4–5 large dried red chillies
500 g (1 lb) raw prawns
1.5 litres water
1 red onion, roughly chopped
5 cm (2 inch) piece galangal, peeled and roughly chopped
4 stems lemon grass (white part only), sliced
3 medium-sized red chillies, seeded and roughly chopped
10 candlenuts
2 teaspoons shrimp paste
2 teaspoons grated fresh turmeric
3 tablespoons oil
2 cups (500 ml/16 fl oz) coconut milk
8 ready-made fried fish balls, sliced
500 g (1 lb) fresh thin rice noodles, gently separated using your fingertips
1–2 Lebanese cucumbers, cut into short, thin strips
100 g ($3^{1}/_{3}$ oz) bean sprouts, scraggly ends removed
$^{1}/_{2}$ cup (10 g/$^{1}/_{3}$ oz) Vietnamese mint leaves

1 Soak the chillies in hot water for 20 minutes, while preparing the stock.

2 Set aside 4 prawns and peel the remainder, retaining all the heads, shells, tails and legs. Place all the peelings in a large, deep heavy-based pan and cook uncovered, over medium heat for 10 minutes, shaking the pan occasionally. The prawn peelings will turn a bright dark orange and become aromatic. Stir in 1 cup (250 ml/8 fl oz) of the water and when it has boiled and almost evaporated away, add another cup and bring it to the boil before adding the remaining water. By slowly adding the water in the initial stages, the colour of the stock will be dark and rich and all the flavour from the base of the pan will be incorporated in the stock. Bring the stock to the boil and simmer gently, uncovered, for 30 minutes. Add the 4 reserved whole prawns and cook until they turn pink; remove with a slotted spoon and set aside. Strain the stock and discard all the peelings. There should be about 2–3 cups (500–750 ml/16–24 fl oz) of stock.

3 While the stock is simmering, drain the chillies and place in a food processor with the onion, galangal, lemon grass, fresh chillies, candlenuts, shrimp paste, turmeric and 2 tablespoons of the oil. Process, wiping down the sides of the bowl regularly with a spatula, until very finely chopped.

4 Heat the remaining oil in a wok and cook the paste over low heat for about 8 minutes, stirring regularly, until the mixture is very aromatic. Stir in the stock and coconut milk. Bring to the boil, lower the heat and simmer for 5 minutes. Add the prawn meat and fish ball slices and simmer until the prawns turn pink.

5 In a separate pan of boiling water, cook the rice noodles for about 30 seconds — don't overcook them or they'll fall apart. Drain well and divide the noodles among 4 deep soup bowls.

6 Ladle the hot soup over the noodles. Garnish with a little of the cucumber, bean sprouts and mint leaves and top each bowl with a cooked prawn. Serve immediately. Arrange the remaining garnishes on a plate so your guests can add more of their favourite to the Laksa.

Soak the large red chillies in hot water for 20 minutes.

Boil the first cup of water until almost evaporated, before adding another cup.

Pour the stock through a strainer or large colander and discard the peelings.

COOK'S FILE

Notes: If fresh thin rice noodles are not available, use dried rice noodles instead and cook according to the directions on the packet.

- A Malay wok, called a 'kauli', is a very heavy wok made from a thick cast-iron type of material. Any heavy-based wok or pan can be used.
- Ready-made fish balls and candlenuts are available at Asian food stores. Candlenuts are used to thicken and flavour curries. Please note that they are thought to be toxic if uncooked. Macadamia nuts can be used instead.

Place the ingredients in a food processor and process until very finely chopped.

Add the prawn meat and fish ball slices and cook until the prawns turn pink.

Cook the rice noodles in rapidly boiling water for about 30 seconds.

BEEF COCONUT CURRY

Preparation time: 1 hour
+ 30 minutes standing
Total cooking time: 2 hours
Serves 4

350 g (11¼ oz) piece round steak
6 dried red chillies
1½ cups (135 g/4½ oz) desiccated coconut
1 medium onion, roughly chopped
3 cloves garlic
2 stems lemon grass (white part only), sliced
3 cm (1¼ cm) piece galangal, sliced
2 cm (¾ inch) piece of fresh ginger, sliced
1 tablespoon ground coriander
2 teaspoons ground cumin
1 teaspoon ground or grated fresh turmeric
1 teaspoon shrimp paste
1 teaspoon grated lime rind
3 tablespoons oil
1 cup (250 ml/8 fl oz) coconut milk
1 tablespoon kecap manis
1 tablespoon tamarind concentrate
¼ teaspoon salt
2 spring onions, very finely sliced, to garnish

1 Cover the steak with water in a medium-sized pan. Bring to the boil, cover and simmer over low heat for 1½ hours. Place the chillies in a bowl, cover with boiling water and soak for 15 minutes. Meanwhile, spread the coconut on an oven tray and toast in a slow 150°C (200°F/Gas 2) oven for 10 minutes or until golden, shaking the tray occasionally. Remove from the tray to prevent burning, set aside.

2 Drain the chillies and place in a food processor with the onion, garlic, lemon grass, galangal, ginger, coriander, cumin, turmeric, shrimp paste and lime rind. Process, adding up to 2 tablespoons of the oil to assist blending, and regularly scraping down the sides of the bowl with a spatula, until the mixture is finely chopped and smooth. Transfer to a bowl; set aside.

3 Remove the meat from the liquid and allow to cool for 20 minutes. Cut the meat into small rectangles. If time is short, wear rubber gloves and cut the meat while hot. Mix the meat with the paste and marinate for 10 minutes.

4 Heat the remaining oil in a wok or heavy-based frying pan and cook the meat mixture over high heat until browned. Add the coconut milk, kecap manis, tamarind and salt; stir for 8 minutes or until the mixture is almost dry. Add the toasted coconut to the wok and toss thoroughly. Garnish with spring onion and serve with steamed rice and a vegetable salad.

Toast the coconut on a tray, in a slow oven, until dark golden.

Combine the meat and marinade paste in a bowl and set aside for 10 minutes.

Add the toasted coconut to the wok and toss until well distributed.

FISH CURRY

Preparation time: 25 minutes
Total cooking time: 25 minutes
Serves 4

3–6 medium-sized red chillies
1 onion, chopped
4 cloves garlic
3 stems lemon grass (white part only), sliced
4 cm (1½ inch) piece of fresh ginger, sliced
2 teaspoons shrimp paste
¼ cup (60 ml/2 fl oz) oil
1 tablespoon fish curry powder
1 cup (250 ml/8 fl oz) coconut milk
1 cup (250 ml/8 fl oz) water
1 tablespoon tamarind concentrate
1 tablespoon kecap manis
350 g (11¼ oz) firm white fish fillets, cut into bite-sized pieces
2 ripe tomatoes, chopped
1 tablespoon lemon juice
¼ teaspoon each salt and pepper

1 Combine the chillies, onion, garlic, lemon grass, ginger and shrimp paste in a small food processor and process until roughly chopped. Add 2 tablespoons of oil, to assist the blending, and process until the mixture forms a smooth paste, regularly scraping down the sides of the bowl with a spatula.

2 Heat the remaining oil in a wok or deep, heavy-based frying pan and add the paste. Cook for 3–4 minutes over low heat, stirring constantly until very fragrant. Add the curry powder and stir for another 2 minutes. Add the coconut milk, water, tamarind and kecap manis to the wok. Bring to the boil, stirring occasionally, then reduce the heat and simmer for 10 minutes.

3 Add the fish, tomato, lemon juice and season with the salt and pepper. Simmer for 5 minutes or until the fish is just cooked. Serve immediately with steamed rice, garnished with sprouts or herbs.

COOK'S FILE

Note: Fish curry powder is a blend of spices suited to seafood flavours. It is available from Asian food stores.

Stir the paste with a wooden spoon, over low heat, for 3–4 minutes.

Simmer the mixture for 10 minutes, stirring occasionally.

Add the fish, tomato and lemon juice and season with salt and pepper.

INDONESIA

BAKED SPICED FISH CUTLETS

Preparation time: 15 minutes
Total cooking time: 15–20 minutes
Serves 4

1 tablespoon oil
1 onion, very finely chopped
2 cloves garlic, finely chopped
5 cm (2 inch) piece of fresh ginger, finely grated
1 teaspoon ground coriander
1 stem lemon grass (white part only), finely chopped
2 teaspoons tamarind concentrate
2 teaspoons very finely grated lemon rind
4 small fish cutlets
lime wedges, to garnish

1 Preheat the oven to warm 160°C (325°F/Gas 3). Line a baking dish or tray with aluminium foil and lightly oil, to prevent the fish from sticking. Heat the oil in a frying pan, add the onion, garlic, ginger, coriander and lemon grass, and stir over medium heat for 5 minutes or until aromatic.

2 Stir in the tamarind, lemon rind and some freshly ground black pepper. Remove from the heat and set aside until cool.

3 Spread the spice paste over the fish; arrange in the dish, in a single layer.

4 Bake for 10–15 minutes, or until the flesh flakes when tested with a fork. Be sure not to overcook the fish or it will be dry. Garnish with lime wedges and serve with steamed rice.

COOK'S FILE

Storage time: The spice mixture can be made one day in advance and refrigerated in an airtight container.
Hint: Adjust the cooking time if the cutlets are particularly thick.

Grate the ginger, using a metal, wooden or ceramic grater.

Fry the onion, garlic, ginger, coriander and lemon grass until aromatic.

Add the tamarind, lemon rind and ground black pepper to the pan.

Spread the spice paste over the top of the fish cutlets.

NASI GORENG
(Fried Rice)

Preparation time: 35 minutes
Total cooking time: 25–30 minutes
Serves 4

2 eggs
1/4 teaspoon salt
1/3 cup (80 ml/2 3/4 fl oz) oil
3 cloves garlic, finely chopped
1 brown onion, finely chopped
2 red chillies, seeded and finely chopped
1 teaspoon dried shrimp paste
1 teaspoon coriander seeds
1/2 teaspoon sugar
200 g (6 1/2 oz) rump steak, finely sliced into small pieces
200 g (6 1/2 oz) raw prawn meat
3 cups (555 g/1 lb 1 3/4 oz) cold, cooked rice
2 teaspoons kecap manis
1 tablespoon soy sauce
4 spring onions, finely chopped
1/2 lettuce, finely shredded
1 cucumber, sliced and halved
3 tablespoons crisp fried onions

1 Beat the eggs and salt until foamy. Heat a frying pan over medium heat and lightly brush with 1 tablespoon oil. Pour about one-quarter of the egg mixture into the pan and cook for 1–2 minutes until the omelette sets. Flip and cook for 30 seconds. Remove from the pan and repeat with the remaining egg mixture. When the omelettes are cold, gently roll up and shred into fine strips; set aside.
2 In a food processor or mortar and pestle, combine garlic, onion, chillies, shrimp paste, coriander and sugar; process or pound until a paste forms.
3 Heat a wok or large deep frying pan over high heat, add 1 tablespoon of the oil and fry the paste for 1 minute or until fragrant. Add the steak and prawns and stir-fry until they change colour.
4 Increase the heat and, when the wok is hot, add the remaining oil and the cold rice. Stir-fry, breaking up any lumps, until the rice is heated through. Add the kecap manis, soy sauce and spring onion; stir-fry for another minute.
5 Arrange lettuce around outside of a large platter. Place the rice in the centre; garnish with omelette strips, cucumber and crisp fried onions.

Remove the omelette from the pan using a spatula.

Process the garlic, onion, chillies, shrimp paste, coriander and sugar into a paste.

Quickly stir-fry the beef and prawn meat until they change colour.

Stir-fry the rice, breaking up any lumps with a wooden spoon.

AYAM PANGGANG
(Spicy Roast Chicken)

Preparation time: 20 minutes
Total cooking time: 55 minutes–1 hour
Serves 4–6

1.5 kg (3 lb) chicken
3 teaspoons chopped chillies
3 cloves garlic, peeled

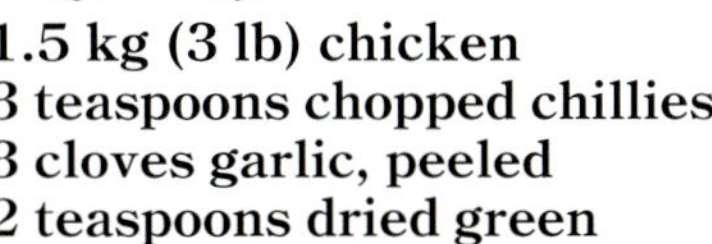

2 teaspoons dried green peppercorns, crushed
2 teaspoons soft brown sugar
2 tablespoons soy sauce
2 teaspoons ground turmeric
1 tablespoon lime juice
30 g (1 oz) butter, chopped

1 Preheat the oven to moderate 180°C (350°F/Gas 4). Using a large cleaver, cut the chicken in half by cutting down the backbone and along the breastbone. To prevent the wings burning, tuck them underneath. Place the chicken, skin-side-up, on a rack in a baking dish and bake for 30 minutes.

2 Meanwhile, combine the chillies, garlic, peppercorns and sugar in a small food processor or mortar and pestle and process briefly, or pound, until smooth. Add the soy sauce, turmeric and lime juice, and process in short bursts until combined.

3 Brush the spice mixture all over the chicken, dot with the butter pieces and bake for another 25–30 minutes or until thoroughly cooked. Serve warm or at room temperature, garnished with lime wedges and fresh herbs, if you like.

Cut the chicken in half by cutting down the backbone and along the breastbone.

Combine the chillies, garlic, peppercorns and brown sugar in a food processor.

Brush the spice mixture all over the chicken and bake until cooked through.

GADO GADO (Vegetables with Peanut Sauce)

Preparation time: 50 minutes
Total cooking time: 20 minutes
Serves 4

250 g (8 oz) potatoes
2 medium carrots
200 g (6½ oz) green beans, topped and tailed
¼ cabbage, shredded
3 hard-boiled eggs, peeled
200 g (6½ oz) bean sprouts, scraggly tails removed
½ telegraph cucumber, sliced
150 g (4¾ oz) firm tofu, cut into cubes
½ cup (80 g/2⅔ oz) roasted peanuts, roughly chopped

Peanut Sauce
1 tablespoon oil
1 large onion, very finely chopped
2 cloves garlic, finely chopped
2 red chillies, very finely chopped
1 teaspoon shrimp paste, optional
250 g (8 oz) crunchy peanut butter
1 cup (250 ml/8 fl oz) coconut milk
1 cup (250 ml/8 fl oz) water
2 teaspoons kecap manis
1 tablespoon tomato sauce

1 Peel the potatoes, cut into thick slices, place in a medium pan, cover with cold water and bring to the boil. Reduce the heat and simmer for about 6 minutes or until just tender. Drain, allow to cool.

2 Cut the carrot into thick slices and the beans into 4 cm (1½ inch) lengths. Bring a large pan of water to the boil, add the carrot slices and beans and cook for 2–3 minutes. Remove with a sieve and plunge the vegetables into a bowl of iced water.

3 Quickly plunge the shredded cabbage into the boiling water for about 20 seconds. Remove from the pan and plunge in the cold water. Drain the vegetables very well.

4 Cut the eggs in quarters or halves. Arrange the potato and carrot slices, beans, shredded cabbage, bean sprouts, cucumber and tofu decoratively on a large serving platter. Cover with plastic wrap and refrigerate while making the sauce.

5 To make Peanut Sauce: Heat the oil in a heavy-based pan, cook the onion and garlic for 8 minutes over low heat, stirring regularly. Add the chillies and shrimp paste to the pan and cook for another minute. Remove the pan from the heat and mix in the peanut butter. Return to the heat and slowly stir in the combined coconut milk and water. Bring the sauce to the boil, stirring constantly over low heat, being careful the sauce does not stick and burn. Add the kecap manis and tomato sauce; simmer for another minute. Allow to cool.

6 Drizzle a little of the Peanut Sauce over the salad, garnish with the chopped peanuts and serve the remaining sauce separately.

COOK'S FILE

Hint: Fresh peanut butter, available from health food stores, will give the best flavour in the sauce. Store any leftover Peanut Sauce in an airtight container in the refrigerator, for up to a week.

Cut the block of tofu vertically, and then cut into small cubes.

Cover the potato slices with cold water in a medium pan.

After cooking the carrots and beans, plunge them into iced water.

Add the chillies and shrimp paste to the onions and garlic in the pan.

Slowly stir in the combined coconut milk and water.

Add the tomato sauce and kecap manis to the mixture and stir well.

MEE GORENG

Preparation time: 45 minutes
Total cooking time: 10 minutes
Serves 4

- 1 large brown onion, finely chopped
- 2 cloves garlic, finely chopped
- 2 red chillies, seeded and finely chopped
- 2 cm (3/4 inch) piece of fresh ginger, grated
- 1/4 cup (60 ml/2 fl oz) oil
- 350 g (11 1/4 oz) Hokkien noodles, gently pulled apart
- 500 g (1 lb) raw prawn meat
- 250 g (8 oz) rump steak, finely sliced
- 4 spring onions, chopped
- 1 large carrot, cut into matchsticks
- 2 celery sticks, cut into matchsticks
- 1 tablespoon kecap manis
- 1 tablespoon soy sauce
- 1 tablespoon tomato sauce
- extra spring onions, to garnish

1 Combine the chopped onion, garlic, chillies and ginger in a small food processor or mortar and pestle. Process in short bursts, or pound, until a paste forms, adding a little of the oil to help the grinding, if necessary. Set aside.

2 Heat 1 tablespoon of the oil in a large wok; stir-fry the noodles until plump and warmed through. Place on a serving plate; cover to keep warm.

3 Add another tablespoon of oil to the wok and stir-fry the paste mixture until golden. Add the prawn meat, steak and vegetables, and stir-fry for 2–3 minutes. Add the kecap manis, soy and tomato sauces, and season well with salt and pepper.

4 Carefully spoon the prawn and vegetable mixture over the noodles and garnish with the extra spring onion. Serve immediately.

Gently prise apart the Hokkien noodles before heating in the wok.

Stir-fry the noodles in the wok until warmed through.

Heat the oil in the wok and stir-fry the paste mixture until golden.

Add the kecap manis, soy and tomato sauces to the wok.

COOK'S FILE

Hint: Hokkien noodles are thick yellow noodles — if they are not available, dried egg noodles may be used, but they must be cooked and well drained.

CREAMY VEGETABLE CURRY

Preparation time: 30 minutes
Total cooking time: 25 minutes
Serves 4

2 tablespoons oil
1 large red onion, roughly chopped
3 cloves garlic, finely chopped
4 red chillies, finely chopped
1 teaspoon shrimp paste
2 fresh bay leaves, torn
1 cup (250 ml/8 fl oz) coconut milk
1 tablespoon tamarind concentrate
2 teaspoons sugar
1/4 teaspoon salt
500 g (1 lb) combined chopped pumpkin, potato and carrot
250 g (8 oz) combined chopped green beans, baby squash or zucchini
2 large tomatoes, peeled and roughly chopped
150 g (4 3/4 oz) baby spinach leaves
2 tablespoons desiccated coconut
2 tablespoons lemon juice

1 Heat the oil in a large heavy-based pan. Add the onion, garlic, chillies and shrimp paste, and cook for 5 minutes, stirring regularly to mix in the shrimp paste. Add the bay leaves, coconut milk, tamarind, sugar and salt. Bring to the boil, reduce the heat and simmer for 5 minutes.

2 Add the pumpkin, potato and carrot. Cover and cook for 7 minutes, stirring occasionally. Add the beans and squash and cook for another 5 minutes or until vegetables are tender. Stir in the tomatoes and spinach and cook, uncovered, for 2 minutes.

3 Just before serving, stir in the coconut and sprinkle with lemon juice. Serve with steamed rice.

COOK'S FILE

Hint: If the curry becomes too thick, add 1/2 cup (125 ml/4 fl oz) of water.

Chop all the vegetables into pieces of a similar size.

When the coconut milk mixture boils, reduce heat and simmer for 5 minutes.

Test the vegetables for tenderness before adding the tomatoes and spinach.

LAOS & CAMBODIA

PRAWNS STEAMED IN BANANA LEAVES

Preparation time: 30 minutes
Total cooking time: 15 minutes
+ 2 hours marinating
Serves 4

2.5 cm (1 inch) piece of fresh ginger, grated
2 small red chillies, finely chopped
4 spring onions, finely chopped
2 stems lemon grass (white part only), finely chopped
2 teaspoons soft brown sugar
1 tablespoon fish sauce
2 tablespoons lime juice
1 tablespoon sesame seeds, toasted
2 tablespoons chopped fresh coriander
1 kg (2 lb) raw prawns, peeled and deveined
8 small banana leaves

1 Process the ginger, chillies, spring onion and lemon grass in a food processor, in short bursts, until the mixture forms a paste. Transfer the paste to a bowl, stir in the sugar, fish sauce, lime juice, sesame seeds and coriander and mix well. Add the prawns and toss to coat. Cover, refrigerate and marinate for 2 hours.

2 Soak the banana leaves in boiling water for 3 minutes to soften. Drain, pat dry and use scissors to cut them into squares of about 18 cm (7 inches).

3 Divide the prawn mixture into eight, place a portion onto each banana leaf, fold the leaf up to enclose the mixture and then secure the parcels, using a bamboo skewer.

4 Cook the parcels in a bamboo steamer over simmering water for 8–10 minutes, or until the prawn filling is cooked.

COOK'S FILE

Notes: Banana leaves are available from Asian food stores and speciality fruit and vegetable shops.

- The parcels can be cooked on the barbecue.
- If the banana leaves are large ones, bigger parcels can be made.
- If banana leaves are not available, the prawn mixture can be wrapped in aluminium foil or baking paper and steamed. If you are cooking them on a barbecue, use foil.

Storage time: The filled parcels can be made up a day beforehand and stored, covered, in the refrigerator.

Use scissors to cut the banana leaves into squares, approximately 18 cm (7 inches).

Enclose the filling and secure the parcel with a bamboo skewer.

FISH AND NOODLE SOUP

Preparation time: 15 minutes
Total cooking time: 20 minutes
Serves 4

200 g (6½ oz) dried rice vermicelli
1 tablespoon oil
2.5 cm (1 inch) piece of fresh ginger, grated
3 small red chillies, finely chopped
4 spring onions, chopped
800 ml (26 fl oz) coconut milk
2 tablespoons fish sauce
2 tablespoons tomato purée
500 g (1 lb) white fish fillets, cut into 2 cm (¾ inch) cubes
2 ham steaks, chopped into small cubes
150 g (4¾ oz) snake beans, cut into short lengths
2 cups (180 g/5¾ oz) bean sprouts, scraggly ends removed
1 cup (20 g/⅔ oz) fresh mint leaves
½ cup (80 g/2⅔ oz) unsalted roasted peanuts

1 Soak the rice vermicelli in boiling water for 5 minutes, then drain.
2 Heat the oil in a large, heavy-based pan, add the ginger, chillies and spring onion and cook over medium heat for 3 minutes, or until onion is golden.
3 Stir in the coconut milk, fish sauce and tomato purée, cover and simmer for 10 minutes.
4 Add the fish cubes, ham and snake beans to the pan and simmer for 10 minutes, or until the fish is tender. Divide the rice vermicelli among deep soup bowls, top with the bean sprouts and mint leaves. Carefully spoon the soup into the bowls and sprinkle with roasted peanuts.

Soak the rice vermicelli in boiling water for 5 minutes.

Cook the ginger, chillies and spring onion over medium heat.

Stir in the coconut milk, fish sauce and tomato purée.

Add the fish pieces, ham and chopped snake beans to the pan.

COOK'S FILE

Storage time: The stock mixture can be made ahead of time. When required, reheat gently, add the fish, ham and vegetables and follow the instructions in the recipe.
Variation: Fresh egg noodles are a good substitute for the rice vermicelli. Cook them in boiling water for 5 minutes. Drain and divide among the bowls.

CHICKEN MINCE WITH HERBS AND SPICES

Preparation time: 30 minutes
Total cooking time: 50 minutes
Serves 4–6

1/4 cup (50 g/1 2/3 oz) long-grain rice
1 kg (2 lb) chicken thigh fillets
2 tablespoons peanut oil
4 cloves garlic, crushed
2 tablespoons grated fresh galangal
2 small red chillies, finely chopped
4 spring onions, finely chopped
1/4 cup (60 ml/2 fl oz) fish sauce
1 tablespoon shrimp paste
3 tablespoons chopped fresh Vietnamese mint
2 tablespoons chopped fresh basil
4 tablespoons lime juice
200 g (6 1/2 oz) chicken livers, optional

1 Spread the rice on an oven tray and then roast it in a moderate 180°C (350°F/Gas 4) oven for 15 minutes or until golden. Cool slightly and process in a food processor until finely ground.

2 Meanwhile, process the chicken in a food processor until finely minced. Heat the oil in a wok or frying pan, add the garlic, galangal, chillies and spring onion and cook over medium heat for 3 minutes or until golden.

3 Add the chicken to the wok and stir for 5 minutes or until browned. Break up any large lumps with a wooden spoon. Stir in the fish sauce and shrimp paste, bring to the boil, reduce the heat and simmer for 5 minutes.

4 Remove from the heat, stir in the herbs, rice and lime juice and mix until well combined. If chicken livers are used, they should be cooked in 1/2 cup (125 ml/4 fl oz) of chicken stock for 5 minutes, or until tender, and then allowed to cool slightly before chopping. Fold them through at this stage. Garnish with split chillies. Serve with sticky rice.

Roast the uncooked rice on an oven tray for 15 minutes or until lightly golden.

Process the chicken thigh fillets in a food processor until finely minced.

Stir-fry the minced chicken in the wok, until browned.

CHICKEN AND PUMPKIN STEW

Preparation time: 30 minutes
Total cooking time: 50 minutes
Serves 4–6

1/2 cup (100 g/3 1/3 oz) long-grain rice
2 tablespoons oil
1 kg (2 lb) chicken pieces
3 cloves garlic, crushed
3 tablespoons finely chopped lemon grass (white part only)
2 teaspoons grated fresh turmeric or 1 teaspoon ground
2 tablespoons grated galangal
6 kaffir lime leaves, finely shredded
6 spring onions, chopped
4 cups (1 litre) chicken stock
500 g (1 lb) pumpkin, cubed
1 small green pawpaw, peeled and chopped
125 g (4 oz) snake beans, cut into short lengths

1 Spread the rice on an oven tray and then roast it in a moderate 180°C (350°F/Gas 4) oven for 15 minutes or until golden. Cool slightly and process in a food processor until finely ground.

2 Meanwhile, heat the oil in a large pan and cook the chicken pieces, in batches, for 5 minutes or until brown. Drain each batch on paper towels.

3 Add the garlic, chopped lemon grass, turmeric, galangal, kaffir lime leaves and spring onion to the pan; cook over medium heat for 3 minutes or until the spring onion is golden. Return the chicken to the pan, add the stock, cover and simmer for 20 minutes. Add the pumpkin and pawpaw and simmer for 10 minutes. Add the beans and simmer for another 10 minutes, or until the chicken is tender. Stir in the ground rice, bring to the boil, reduce the heat and simmer for 5 minutes or until the mixture thickens slightly. Garnish with kaffir lime leaves.

Cook batches of chicken pieces in a large pan until brown.

Add the pumpkin and green pawpaw pieces to the pan.

Add the ground rice to the mixture and stir well.

LAOTIAN DRIED BEEF WITH GREEN PAWPAW SALAD

Preparation time: 40 minutes
+ 4 hours marinating
Total cooking time: 5 hours
Serves 6

1 kg (2 lb) piece of topside steak, partially frozen
2 teaspoons salt
1/4 teaspoon chilli powder
1 teaspoon ground black pepper
1 tablespoon soft brown sugar
4 cloves garlic, crushed
2 teaspoons sesame oil
1 tablespoon peanut oil

Green Pawpaw Salad
1 small green pawpaw, peeled and seeds removed
1 carrot
2 cloves garlic, crushed
6 cm (2 1/2 inch) piece of fresh ginger, grated
2 small red chillies, finely chopped
2 tablespoons fish sauce
4 kaffir lime leaves, finely shredded
1 tablespoon lime juice
2 teaspoons soft brown sugar
1 teaspoon sesame oil
1 cup (30 g/1 oz) fresh coriander leaves
1 cup (160 g/5 1/4 oz) roasted unsalted peanuts

1 Trim any excess fat from the topside steak, cut the steak into 2.5 mm (1/8 inch) thick slices and then cut into strips. Mix the salt, chilli powder, pepper, sugar, garlic, sesame oil and peanut oil in a bowl. Add the steak and, using your fingertips, toss it in the oil mixture until well coated. Cover, refrigerate and marinate for 4 hours.

2 Place meat on racks in a baking dish; cook in very slow 120°C (250°F/Gas 1/2) oven for 5 hours, or until dried.

3 Warm the beef under a hot grill for 3 minutes, before serving. Serve with Green Pawpaw Salad.

4 To make Green Pawpaw Salad: Cut the green pawpaw and the carrot into fine shreds, using a citrus zester or a sharp knife. Combine in a bowl with the remaining ingredients and toss lightly until mixed. Serve immediately.

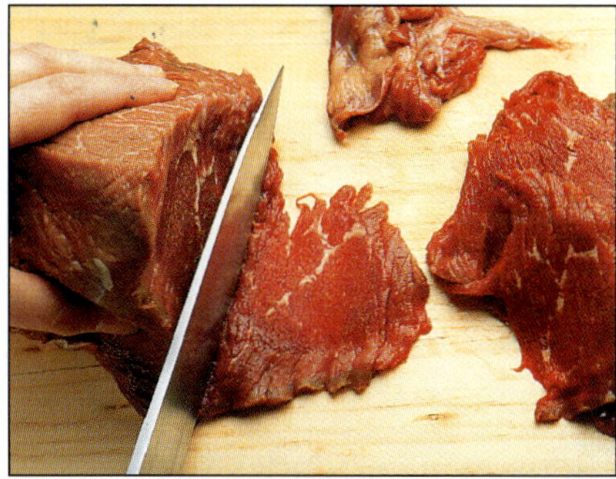

Trim the steak of excess fat and then slice it into very thin slices.

Use your fingertips to thoroughly coat the steak with the oil mixture.

Place the meat strips onto racks and cook in a very slow oven until beef is dried.

Shred the green pawpaw, using a citrus zester, if you have one.

SPICY ROAST CHICKEN

Preparation time: 30 minutes
Total cooking time: 1 hour 20 minutes
Serves 6

3 small dried red chillies
1 teaspoon fennel seeds
1 teaspoon cumin seeds
1 teaspoon coriander seeds
1/8 teaspoon salt
1.5 kg (3 lb) chicken
2 cloves garlic, crushed
1 tablespoon peanut oil
2 onions, chopped
250 g (8 oz) pork mince
1/2 cup (80 g/2 2/3 oz) peanuts, roasted and roughly chopped
3 tablespoons lime juice
1 tablespoon chopped fresh mint
2 tablespoons chopped fresh coriander leaves
1 teaspoon oil, extra
1/2 cup (125 ml/4 fl oz) coconut milk

1 Preheat the oven to moderate 180°C (350°F/Gas 4). Place the red chillies, fennel, cumin, coriander seeds and salt in a small food processor or mortar and pestle and process or grind until the spices are blended to a powder.
2 Remove any excess fat from the chicken and rub the skin and inside cavity with the crushed garlic.
3 Heat the oil in a wok, add the onion and cook over medium heat for 3 minutes or until golden. Add the pork mince and cook for 10 minutes or until the pork is brown. Remove from the heat, stir in the chopped peanuts, lime juice, mint and coriander. Allow the mixture to cool slightly before stuffing the chicken. Tightly secure the opening with a wooden skewer and tie the legs together with some kitchen string.
4 Brush the outside of the chicken lightly with oil and then rub the skin with the spice mixture. Place the chicken on a rack in a baking dish. Bake for 30 minutes. Remove the chicken from the oven and baste with coconut milk and pan juices. Bake for another 40 minutes, basting frequently until the chicken is tender. Remove the skewer and string before serving. A garnish of fresh herbs makes the chicken look attractive.

Grind the chillies, fennel, coriander, cumin and salt until they form a powder.

Cook the chopped onion in the wok until soft and golden.

Spoon the prepared filling into the cavity of the chicken.

Rub the spice mixture all over the surface of the chicken, using your fingers.

SEAFOOD SOUP

Preparation time: 30 minutes
Total cooking time: 40 minutes
Serves 6

1 tablespoon oil
5 cm (2 inch) piece of fresh ginger, grated
3 tablespoons finely chopped lemon grass (white part only)
3 small red chillies, finely chopped
2 onions, chopped
4 medium tomatoes, peeled, seeded and chopped
3 cups (750 ml/24 fl oz) good-quality fish stock
3 cups (750 ml/24 fl oz) water
4 kaffir lime leaves, finely shredded
1 cup (160 g/5¼ oz) chopped fresh pineapple
1 tablespoon tamarind concentrate
1 tablespoon grated palm sugar
2 tablespoons lime juice
1 tablespoon fish sauce
500 g (1 lb) white fish fillets, cut into small cubes
500 g (1 lb) raw medium prawns, peeled
2 tablespoons chopped fresh coriander

1 Heat the oil in a large pan, add the ginger, lemon grass, chillies and onion and stir over medium heat for 5 minutes or until the onion is golden.

2 Add the tomato to the pan and cook for 3 minutes. Stir in the fish stock, water, kaffir lime leaves, pineapple, tamarind, palm sugar, lime juice and fish sauce; cover and bring to the boil. Reduce the heat and simmer for 15 minutes.

3 Add the fish, prawns and coriander to the pan and simmer for 10 minutes or until the seafood is tender.

COOK'S FILE

Storage time: The stock for this recipe can be made in advance and frozen in an airtight container.

Note: Buy tamarind concentrate and palm sugar at Asian food stores.

Use a sharp knife to finely shred the kaffir lime leaves.

Stir the ginger, lemon grass, chillies and onion until golden.

Add the pineapple to the pan, cover and bring the mixture to the boil.

SPICY FRIED FISH

Preparation time: 20 minutes
Total cooking time: 20 minutes
Serves 6

1 cup (125 g/4 oz) plain flour
1 teaspoon ground cumin
1 teaspoon ground coriander
1 teaspoon ground paprika
750 g ($1\frac{1}{2}$ lb) firm, white fish fillets such as Ling
2 egg whites, lightly beaten
oil, for deep-frying

Sauce
1 teaspoon sesame oil
2 cloves garlic, crushed
2.5 cm (1 inch) piece of fresh ginger, grated
1 onion, sliced
4 spring onions, cut into short lengths
1 tablespoon fish sauce
2 tablespoons low-salt soy sauce
1 tablespoon soft brown sugar
1 cup (250 ml/8 fl oz) water
1 tablespoon cornflour

1 Mix the flour, ground cumin, coriander and paprika in a medium-sized bowl. Cut the fish fillets into 2 cm ($\frac{3}{4}$ inch) cubes. Dip the cubes in the egg white and dust lightly with the flour mixture, shaking off any excess.

2 Heat the oil in a deep pan or wok and deep-fry the fish pieces, in batches, over high heat for 3–4 minutes or until golden and cooked through. Drain on paper towels and keep warm.

3 To make Sauce: Heat the sesame oil in a pan. Add the garlic, ginger, onion and spring onion and cook over medium heat for 3 minutes or until the onion is golden. Stir in the fish and soy sauces, brown sugar and water. Dissolve the cornflour in a little water and add to the sauce mixture, stirring constantly until the mixture boils and thickens.

4 Serve the fish pieces topped with the hot sauce. Garnish with sliced spring onion. Steamed rice or a salad would be a suitable accompaniment.

Dip the fish cubes in the egg white and dust lightly with the flour.

Deep-fry the coated fish in hot oil, in batches, until golden and cooked.

Add the dissolved cornflour to the sauce and stir thoroughly until thickened.

When the char-grilled steak has been set aside for 5 minutes, cut it into thin slices.

Cook the sliced beef in the hot water, over medium heat, for 2 minutes.

Add the lemon juice, lemon grass, fish sauce, onion, coriander and mint to meat.

Shred the Chinese cabbage, using a large, sharp knife or cleaver.

MARINATED BEEF SALAD

Preparation time: 20 minutes
Total cooking time: 10 minutes
+ 2 hours marinating
Serves 4

500 g (1 lb) rump steak
4 tablespoons water
3 tablespoons lemon juice
2 tablespoons finely chopped lemon grass (white part only)
1 tablespoon fish sauce
1 onion, finely sliced
2 tablespoons chopped fresh coriander
1 tablespoon chopped fresh mint
2 Lebanese cucumbers, chopped
1/2 Chinese cabbage, shredded

1 Char-grill the steak for 3 minutes on each side or until cooked to medium-rare. Remove, cover and set aside for 5 minutes. Use a sharp knife to cut the steak into 5 mm (1/4 inch) thick slices.

2 Heat the water in a wok, add the sliced beef and cook over medium heat for 2 minutes. Do not overcook. Remove from the heat and transfer the beef and liquid to a bowl.

3 Add the lemon juice, lemon grass, fish sauce, sliced onion, chopped coriander and mint to the beef and mix until well combined. Cover and refrigerate, leaving to marinate for 2 hours. Stir in the cucumber.

4 Serve the beef salad on a bed of shredded cabbage, garnished with extra mint leaves, if you like.

COOK'S FILE

Hint: The meat can be marinated overnight. Add the cucumber just before serving.

PHILIPPINES

PRAWN FRITTERS

Preparation time: 25 minutes
Total cooking time: 15 minutes
Serves 4–6

300 g (9⅔ oz) raw prawns, peeled and deveined
1 egg
¾ cup (185 ml/6 fl oz) water
1 tablespoon fish sauce
1 cup (125 g/4 fl oz) plain flour
¼ teaspoon bagoong (shrimp paste)
3 spring onions, sliced
1 small red chilli, finely chopped
50 g (1⅔ oz) dried rice vermicelli, soaked in boiling water for 5 minutes, drained and cut into short lengths
oil, for deep-frying
dipping sauce (see page 100) or bottled sweet chilli sauce

1 Process half the prawns in a food processor until smooth. Chop the remaining prawns and mix, in a bowl, with the processed prawns.

2 In a small jug, beat the egg, water and fish sauce. Sift the flour into a bowl, make a well in the centre, gradually add the egg mixture and stir until smooth.

3 Add the prawn mixture, bagoong, spring onion, red chillies and rice vermicelli to the bowl and mix until well combined.

4 Heat the oil in a large pan or wok, drop tablespoonsful of mixture in the pan and deep-fry the fritters in batches for 3 minutes or until crisp and golden. Drain on paper towels. Repeat with the remaining mixture. Serve with your choice of dipping sauce.

COOK'S FILE

Variation: Use fish instead of prawns — process in the same way.

Transfer the processed prawns to a bowl, add the chopped prawns and mix.

Gradually add the egg mixture to the flour and stir until smooth.

Add the prawns, bagoong, spring onion, red chillies and rice vermicelli to the bowl.

Drop tablespoonsful of mixture into the hot oil and cook until crisp and golden.

OXTAIL AND VEGETABLE STEW

Preparation time: 30 minutes
Total cooking time: 2 hours 15 minutes
Serves 6

1.5 kg (3 lb) oxtail, cut into 4 cm (3/4 inch) lengths
1/4 cup (45 g/1 1/2 oz) lard
2 tablespoons annatto seeds or 1 tablespoon paprika and 1/2 teaspoon turmeric
2 onions, finely sliced
4 cloves garlic, crushed
6 cups (1.5 litres) water
1 bay leaf
1 tablespoon soy sauce
2 tablespoons fish sauce
2 turnips, peeled and chopped
2 cups (250 g/8 oz) sliced green beans
2 baby eggplants, sliced
2 large sweet potatoes, chopped
1/2 cup (110 g/3 2/3 oz) rice
1/2 cup (80 g/2 2/3 oz) unsalted peanuts

1 Soak the meat in a large pan of salted boiling water for 5 minutes, remove and pat dry. Discard the liquid.
2 Heat the lard in a large pan, add the annatto seeds or spices and cook over medium heat until the lard turns red. (Annatto seeds can be discarded at this point or left in, but not eaten.) Add the onion and garlic to the pan and cook for 5 minutes. Remove and drain on paper towels.
3 Brown the meat in batches in a dry non-stick pan, over medium heat, for 5 minutes. Add the meat to the large pan and add the onion and garlic, water, bay leaf, soy and fish sauces. Bring to the boil, reduce the heat and simmer, covered, for 1 1/2 hours. Add the vegetables and simmer for 20 minutes, or until the vegetables are tender.
4 Spread the rice and peanuts on oven trays and roast in a moderate 180°C (350°F/Gas 4) oven for 15 minutes, or until golden. Remove, allow to cool slightly and then process both in a food processor until the mixture resembles fine breadcrumbs. Sift the mixture to remove any large pieces and then stir it into the stew until the sauce thickens.

Cook the annatto seeds until the lard turns red.

Add the cooked onion and garlic, water, bay leaf, soy and fish sauces to the meat.

Sift the processed, roasted rice and peanuts and discard any large pieces.

RICE WITH CHICKEN AND SEAFOOD

Preparation time: 40 minutes
Total cooking time: 40 minutes
Serves 4–6

500 g (1 lb) raw medium prawns
500 g (1 lb) mussels
200 g (6½ oz) calamari tubes
3 tablespoons oil
2 chorizo sausages, thickly sliced
500 g (1 lb) chicken pieces
300 g (9⅔ oz) pork fillet, thickly sliced
4 cloves garlic, crushed
2 red onions, chopped
¼ teaspoon saffron threads, soaked in hot water
¼ teaspoon turmeric
4 large tomatoes, peeled, seeded and chopped
2 cups (440 g/14 oz) short-grain rice
5 cups (1.25 litres) hot good-quality chicken stock
125 g (4 oz) green beans, cut into 4 cm (1½ inch) lengths
1 red capsicum, cut into thin strips
1 cup (155 g/5 oz) fresh peas

1 Peel the prawns. Devein, leaving tails intact. Scrub the mussels and remove the beards. Cut the calamari tubes into ½ cm (¼ inch) thin slices. Heat 1 tablespoon of oil in a large, heavy-based pan and add the chorizo; cook over medium heat for 5 minutes or until browned. Drain on paper towels. Add the chicken pieces and cook for 5 minutes or until golden, turning once. Drain on paper towels.

2 Add the pork to the pan and cook for 3 minutes or until browned, turning once. Drain on paper towels. Heat the remaining oil in the pan, add the garlic, onion, saffron and turmeric; cook over medium heat 3 minutes or until the onion is soft. Add the tomato; cook for 3 minutes or until soft.

3 Add the rice and stir for 5 minutes, or until the rice is translucent. Stir in the stock, bring to the boil, cover and simmer for 10 minutes. Add the chicken, cover and cook for 20 minutes. Add the pork, prawns, mussels, calamari, chorizo and vegetables; cover and cook for 10 minutes or until liquid is absorbed.

Drain the cooked chorizo sausage slices on paper towels.

Cook the pork slices until browned on both sides.

Add the rice to the pan and cook until the rice is translucent.

CHICKEN ADOBO

Preparation time: 20 minutes + 2 hours marinating
Total cooking time: 1 hour
Serves 6

1.5 kg (3 lb) chicken pieces
6 cloves garlic, crushed
1 cup (250 ml/8 fl oz) cider vinegar
1 1/2 cups (375 ml/12 fl oz) chicken stock
1 bay leaf
1 teaspoon coriander seeds
1 teaspoon black peppercorns
1 teaspoon annatto seeds or 1/4 teaspoon paprika and 1/8 teaspoon turmeric
3 tablespoons soy sauce
2 tablespoons oil

1 Combine all the ingredients, except the oil, in a large bowl. Cover and refrigerate for 2 hours.

2 Transfer the mixture to a large heavy-based pan, bring to the boil over high heat, reduce the heat and simmer, covered, for 30 minutes. Uncover the pan and continue cooking for 10 minutes, or until the chicken is tender. Remove the chicken from the pan and set aside. Bring the liquid back to the boil and cook over high heat for 10 minutes or until reduced by half.

3 Heat the oil in a wok or large non-stick frying pan and add the chicken in batches, cooking over medium heat for 5 minutes, or until crisp and brown. Serve the reduced sauce mixture over the chicken pieces and accompany with rice.

COOK'S FILE

Note: Annatto seeds are available at speciality stores.

Mix the chicken with the marinade and refrigerate, covered, for 2 hours.

After removing the chicken from the pan, boil the liquid until it has reduced by half.

Cook the chicken pieces, in batches, until they are crisp and golden.

Drain the bamboo shoots and cut them into matchsticks.

Whisk the cornflour and plain flour into the egg mixture.

Cook the crepes on both sides until lightly golden. Repeat until all the batter is used.

Fold the sides of the crepe over the filling and roll up to enclose.

PRAWN CREPES

Preparation time: 40 minutes + 20 minutes resting
Total cooking time: 20 minutes
Serves 4–6

5 eggs
1 1/2 cups (375 ml/12 fl oz) water
2 tablespoons oil
1/2 cup (60 g/2 oz) cornflour
1/2 cup (60 g/2 oz) plain flour

Filling
1 tablespoon oil
500 g (1 lb) raw prawns, peeled and deveined
300 g (9 2/3 oz) canned or bottled bamboo shoots, cut into matchsticks
1 cup (90 g/3 oz) bean sprouts
1/2 cup (80 g/2 2/3 oz) peanuts, roasted and roughly chopped
1/2 lettuce, shredded
1 cup (30 g/1 oz) fresh coriander leaves

1 Beat the eggs, water and oil in a bowl until combined. Whisk in the cornflour and plain flour and beat until smooth. Cover and allow the batter to rest for 20 minutes.

2 Brush a small non-stick frying pan or crepe pan with oil and heat over low heat. Add 2 tablespoons of the batter and swirl the pan to ensure the base has a very thin covering; pour any excess batter back into the bowl. Cook the crepe for 2 minutes or until lightly golden. Turn and cook the other side for 2 minutes. Repeat with the remaining batter.

3 To make Filling: Heat the oil in a non-stick pan, add the prawns (cut in half, lengthways, if large) and cook over medium heat for 5 minutes or until bright pink. Have the other filling ingredients ready to use — set them out on plates or a board.

4 Top each crepe with a little shredded lettuce, a few coriander leaves, prawns, bamboo shoots, sprouts and peanuts, fold in the sides and roll up to enclose the mixture.

COOK'S FILE

Variation: Wrap the cooked filling in soft-leaved lettuce leaves instead of crepes.

SINGAPORE

SINGAPORE NOODLES

Preparation time: 35 minutes + soaking
Total cooking time: 15–20 minutes
Serves 2–4

300 g (9½ oz) dried rice vermicelli
2 tablespoons oil
2 cloves garlic, finely chopped
350 g (11¼ oz) pork loin, cut into strips
300 g (9⅔ oz) raw prawn meat
1 large onion, cut into thin wedges
1–2 tablespoons curry powder
155 g (5 oz) green beans, cut into small diagonal pieces
1 large carrot, cut into fine matchsticks
1 teaspoon caster sugar
1 teaspoon salt
1 tablespoon soy sauce
200 g (6½ oz) bean sprouts, scraggly ends removed
spring onion, cut into fine strips, to garnish, optional

1 Soak the dried rice vermicelli in boiling water for 5 minutes, or until soft. Drain well.
2 Heat 1 tablespoon of the oil in a wok and add the garlic, pork and prawn meat. Stir-fry for 2 minutes or until just cooked, then remove from the wok. Reduce the heat to medium.
3 Heat the remaining oil in the wok and add the onion and curry powder; stir-fry for 2–3 minutes. Add the beans, carrot, sugar and salt, sprinkle with a little water and stir-fry for 2 minutes.
4 Add the vermicelli and soy sauce to the wok and toss with 2 wooden spoons. Add the bean sprouts and pork mixture, season with some extra salt, pepper and sugar, to taste, and toss well. Garnish with spring onion.

Soak the rice vermicelli in boiling water for 5 minutes, or until soft.

Stir-fry the onion with the curry powder for 2–3 minutes.

Sprinkle a little water over the vegetables before stir-frying.

Just before serving, add the bean sprouts and pork mixture and toss well.

DEEP-FRIED SPRING ROLLS

Preparation time: 40 minutes
Total cooking time: 25 minutes
Makes 18

2 tablespoons oil
2 cloves garlic, chopped
3 cm (1¼ inch) piece of fresh ginger, grated
100 g (3⅓ oz) pork mince
100 g (3⅓ oz) chicken mince
50 g (1⅔ oz) raw prawn meat, finely chopped
2 teaspoons sesame oil
2 celery sticks, finely chopped
1 small carrot, finely chopped
½ cup (90 g/3 oz) water chestnuts, chopped
4 spring onions, chopped
1 cup (45 g/1½ oz) finely shredded Chinese cabbage
½ cup (125 ml/4 fl oz) chicken stock
1 tablespoon cornflour
2 tablespoons oyster sauce
1 tablespoon soy sauce
½ teaspoon each of salt and white pepper
¼ cup (30 g/1 oz) cornflour, extra
⅓ cup (80 ml/2¾ fl oz) water
36 small spring roll wrappers
oil, for deep-frying
dipping sauce (see page 100) or bottled sweet chilli sauce

1 Heat 1 tablespoon oil in a wok or frying pan, add the garlic and ginger and stir for 30 seconds. Add the pork, chicken and prawn; stir for 3 minutes or until cooked. Transfer to a bowl and stir in the sesame oil. Set aside to cool.

2 Wipe the wok, heat the remaining oil, add the celery, carrot, chestnuts, spring onion and cabbage and stir-fry for about 2 minutes. In a bowl, stir the chicken stock, cornflour, oyster sauce, soy sauce, salt and pepper until smooth. Add to the vegetables; stir until thickened. Stir in the meat mixture.

3 In a small bowl, mix the extra cornflour with the water until smooth. Place 1 spring roll wrapper on a work surface with a corner facing you. Brush all edges with a little cornflour paste and lay a second sheet on top. Brush edges of the second sheet with cornflour paste. Spread 1 tablespoon of the filling across the bottom corner of the wrapper. Fold the bottom corner up over the filling, tuck in the sides and roll up securely. Repeat with the remaining wrappers and filling.

4 Heat the oil in a large pan and cook the rolls, in batches, for 2–3 minutes, until crisp and golden. Drain on paper towels and serve with your choice of dipping sauce.

Chop the water chestnuts into small pieces, using a sharp knife.

Stir-fry the meat, using a wooden spoon, for 3 minutes, or until cooked.

Fold the bottom corner up over the filling, tuck in the sides and then roll up.

NOODLE SOUP

Preparation time: 30 minutes
Total cooking time: 30 minutes
Serves 4

300 g (9 2/3 oz) small cooked prawns
200 g (6 1/2 oz) baby spinach leaves
500 g (1 lb) fresh Shanghai noodles
1 tablespoon oil
1 large brown onion, finely chopped
5 cm (2 inch) piece of fresh ginger, grated
2 red chillies, finely chopped
1.5 litres chicken stock
2 tablespoons soy sauce
2 teaspoons soft brown sugar
6 spring onions, chopped
crisp fried garlic and onion, bean sprouts (scraggly ends removed), dried chilli flakes, chopped garlic chives, sugar, salt and pepper, for serving

1 Peel the prawns leaving the tails intact. Wash and drain the spinach and snap off any long stems; set aside.

2 Add the noodles to boiling water and cook for 3 minutes, or until plump and tender. Drain and set aside. Heat the oil in a large pan, add onion and ginger and cook for 8 minutes over medium heat, stirring regularly.

3 Add the chillies, stock, soy sauce and sugar, bring to the boil, reduce the heat and simmer for 10 minutes; add spring onion. Divide the noodles among large soup bowls, top with prawns and spinach leaves. Pour over the boiling stock and top with a selection of the garnishes. Serve immediately, with any remaining garnishes for guests to add, according to their taste.

Peel all the cooked prawns, leaving the tails intact.

Add the noodles to boiling water and cook for 3 minutes, or until tender.

After simmering the stock mixture for 10 minutes, add the spring onion.

STEAMED COCONUT RICE

Preparation time: 5 minutes + 45 minutes standing
Total cooking time: 1 hour 5 minutes
Serves 4

500 g (1 lb) long-grain white rice
1½ cups (375 ml/12 fl oz) coconut milk
1 teaspoon salt

1 Pour 2 cups (500 ml/16 fl oz) of water into a wok. Place a large sheet of baking paper in the base of a large bamboo steamer and spread the rice in the base of the steamer. Bring the water to the boil, sit the steamer over the wok (it should not touch the water) and put the lid on the steamer. Steam the rice for 35 minutes, turning the rice over halfway through cooking time, and replenishing the water, if necessary.

2 Gently heat the coconut milk, with the salt, in a medium-sized pan. Add the steamed rice, bring to the boil and stir well. Cover with a tight-fitting lid and remove from the heat. Set aside for 45 minutes, or until the coconut milk is absorbed.

3 Spread the rice back into the paper-lined steaming bamboo basket and cover. Check that there is water in the wok and then steam for another 30 minutes.

COOK'S FILE

Note: The result is a chewy, light and delicately-flavoured rice. Jasmine or basmati rice can be used.

Spread the rice in the base of the baking paper-lined bamboo steamer.

Add the steamed rice to the pan of coconut milk.

Allow the rice to stand for 45 minutes until the coconut milk is absorbed.

MIXED VEGETABLE SALAD

Preparation time: 40 minutes + chilling
Total cooking time: 5 minutes
Serves 4–6

300 g (9⅔ oz) chopped fresh pineapple pieces
1 telegraph cucumber, chopped
250 g (8 oz) cherry tomatoes, halved
155 g (5 oz) green beans, finely sliced
155 g (5 oz) bean sprouts, scraggly ends removed
⅓ cup (80 ml/2¾ fl oz) rice wine vinegar
2 tablespoons lime juice
2 red chillies, seeded and finely chopped
2 teaspoons sugar
¼ teaspoon salt
30 g (1 oz) dried small prawns and mint leaves, to garnish

1 In a bowl, combine the pineapple, cucumber, tomatoes, beans and sprouts; toss well, cover and refrigerate until chilled. Stir the vinegar, lime juice, chillies, sugar and salt in a small bowl, until the sugar dissolves.

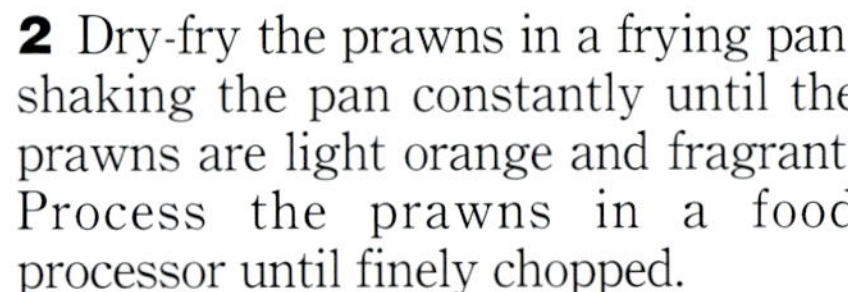

2 Dry-fry the prawns in a frying pan, shaking the pan constantly until the prawns are light orange and fragrant. Process the prawns in a food processor until finely chopped.

3 Arrange the chilled salad on a serving platter, drizzle half the dressing over the top and garnish with the dried prawns and mint leaves. Serve immediately, with the remaining dressing on the side.

COOK'S FILE

Variation: Fresh mango or pawpaw can be used instead of pineapple. Toss gently so you don't break the pieces.

Pull the scraggly ends from the bean sprouts, using your fingers.

Dry-fry the dried small prawns, shaking the pan constantly to prevent burning.

Process the fried prawns until they are finely chopped.

Steamed Coconut Rice (top) and Mixed Vegetable Salad

CHICKEN SATAY WITH PEANUT SAUCE

Preparation time: 40 minutes
+ 30 minutes marinating
Total cooking time: 15–20 minutes
Serves 4

500 g (1 lb) chicken thigh fillets, trimmed
1 onion, roughly chopped
2 stems lemon grass (white part only), thinly sliced
4 cloves garlic
2 red chillies, chopped
2 teaspoons ground coriander
1 teaspoon ground cumin
1/2 teaspoon salt
1 tablespoon soy sauce
1/4 cup (60 ml/2 fl oz) oil
1 tablespoon soft brown sugar
cucumber slices and chopped roasted peanuts, to garnish

Peanut Sauce
1/2 cup (125 g/4 oz) crunchy peanut butter
1 cup (250 ml/8 fl oz) coconut milk
1/2 cup (125 ml/4 fl oz) water
1–2 tablespoons sweet chilli sauce
1 tablespoon soy sauce
2 teaspoons lemon juice

1 Soak 20 wooden skewers in cold water for 30 minutes. Cut the chicken into flattish thick strips about 6 cm (2 1/2 inches) long and 2 cm (1 inch) wide. Thread 1 strip of chicken onto each skewer, flattening it on the skewer.
2 Process the onion, lemon grass, garlic, chillies, coriander, cumin, salt and soy sauce in a food processor, in short bursts, until smooth, adding a little oil to assist the processing. Spread the mixture over the chicken, cover and refrigerate for 30 minutes.
3 To make Peanut Sauce: Stir all the ingredients in a heavy-based pan, over low heat, until the mixture boils. Remove from the heat. The sauce will thicken on standing.
4 Heat a char-grill or barbecue flatplate until very hot and brush with the remaining oil. Cook the chicken for 2–3 minutes on each side, sprinkling with a little oil and brown sugar (this will help produce a lovely flavour and colour). Serve topped with Peanut Sauce and garnished with cucumber slices and chopped peanuts. Serve the remaining Peanut Sauce as a dipping sauce.

Thread one chicken strip onto each skewer, flattening it out on the skewer.

Add a little oil to the paste to assist the processing.

Peanut Sauce will thicken when it has been standing.

During cooking, sprinkle the chicken with oil and brown sugar.

CHILLI CRAB

Preparation time: 55 minutes
Total cooking time: 45 minutes
Serves 2–4

2 very fresh blue swimmer crabs, approximately 500 g (1 lb) each
1/2 cup (60 g/2 oz) flour
1/4 cup (60 ml/2 fl oz) oil
1 medium onion, finely chopped
5 cm (2 inch) piece of fresh ginger, finely grated
4 cloves garlic, finely chopped
3–5 red chillies, finely chopped
2 cups (500 ml/16 fl oz) ready-made tomato pasta sauce
1 cup (250 ml/8 fl oz) water
2 tablespoons soy sauce
2 tablespoons sweet chilli sauce
1 tablespoon rice wine vinegar
2 tablespoons soft brown sugar
dipping sauce (see page 100) or bottled chilli or soy sauce

1 Wash the crabs well and scrub the shells, using a scourer. Using a large cleaver, cut the crabs in half and rinse well under cold water, carefully removing the yellow gills or spongy parts. Hit the legs and larger front nippers with the flat side of the cleaver to crack the shells (to make eating the meat inside easier).

2 Dust the crabs all over with flour; shake off any excess. Heat about 2 tablespoons of the oil in a large wok, cook one crab half at a time, carefully turning and holding the crab in the hot oil until the shell just turns red. Repeat with the remaining crab.

3 Add the remaining oil to the wok, cook the onion, ginger, garlic and chillies for 5 minutes, over medium heat, stirring regularly. Add the tomato sauce, water, soy sauce, chilli sauce, vinegar and brown sugar. Bring to the boil and cook for 15 minutes. Return the crab to the wok and simmer turning carefully in the sauce for 8–10 minutes or until the crab meat turns white. Do not overcook. Serve with steamed rice and your choice of sauces for dipping.

COOK'S FILE

Hint: Provide finger bowls for your guests. Bibs are handy as well.

Hit the legs and larger front nippers to crack the shells.

Turn the crab and hold it in hot oil until the shell turns red.

Add the tomato sauce, water, soy sauce, chilli sauce, vinegar and brown sugar.

DIPPING SAUCES

BASIC DIPPING SAUCE

In a small bowl, dissolve 1 teaspoon sugar in 1/3 cup (80 ml/2 3/4 fl oz) fish sauce, stirring constantly. Add 2 tablespoons rice wine vinegar, 1 tablespoon lime juice and 2 seeded and very finely chopped red chillies. Finely grate 1/2 small peeled carrot and 1 peeled radish and stir them into the sauce just before serving. (The basic sauce, without the vegetables, can be stored, covered, in the refrigerator, for up to 1 week. Serve at room temperature.)
Makes approximately 1/2 cup (125 ml/4 fl oz)

SESAME SEED DIPPING SAUCE

Crush 100 g (3 1/3 oz) toasted Japanese white sesame seeds until they form a paste, using a mortar and pestle or a clean coffee grinder. Add 2 teaspoons of vegetable oil, if necessary, to assist in forming a paste. Mix the paste with 1/2 cup (125 ml/4 fl oz) shoshoyu (Japanese soy sauce), 2 tablespoons mirin, 3 teaspoons caster sugar, 1/2 teaspoon instant dashi granules and 1/2 cup (125 ml/4 fl oz) warm water. Cover and refrigerate. Use within 2 days.
Makes approximately 1 3/4 cups (440 ml/14 fl oz)

Dipping Sauces, clockwise from top left: Soy and Ginger; Lemon and Garlic; Sesame Seed; Basic; Ginger

GINGER DIPPING SAUCE

Peel a 5 cm (2 inch) piece of fresh ginger and grate it very finely. In a small bowl, stir 2 tablespoons each of sugar and rice wine vinegar and 1 tablespoon fish sauce, until the sugar dissolves. Add the ginger, 2 tablespoons chopped fresh coriander and 1 seeded and finely chopped green chilli to the bowl; chill for 15 minutes before serving.
Makes approximately 1/2 cup (125 ml/4 fl oz)

LEMON AND GARLIC DIPPING SAUCE

In a small bowl, stir 1/4 cup (60 ml/2 fl oz) lemon juice, 2 tablespoons fish sauce and 1 tablespoon sugar until the sugar dissolves. Stir in 2 chopped small red chillies and 3 finely chopped cloves of garlic.
Makes approximately 3/4 cup (185 ml/6 fl oz)

SOY AND GINGER DIPPING SAUCE

Combine 1 cup (250 ml/8 fl oz) shoshoyu (Japanese soy sauce), a 5 cm (2 inch) piece of peeled and finely grated fresh ginger and 2 teaspoons caster sugar in a small bowl. Whisk well and serve within 15 minutes of preparation.
Makes 1 cup (250 ml/8 fl oz)

CURRY PASTES

RED CURRY PASTE

1 tablespoon coriander seeds
2 teaspoons cumin seeds
1 teaspoon black peppercorns
2 teaspoons dried shrimp paste
1 teaspoon ground nutmeg
12 large dried or small fresh red chillies, roughly chopped
1 cup (110 g/3 2/3 oz) Asian shallots, chopped
2 tablespoons oil
4 stems lemon grass (white part only), finely chopped
12 small cloves garlic, chopped
2 tablespoons fresh coriander roots, chopped
2 tablespoons fresh coriander stems, chopped
6 kaffir lime leaves, shredded
3 teaspoons paprika
2 teaspoons grated lime rind
2 teaspoons salt
2 teaspoons turmeric

Toast the coriander and cumin seeds in a dry frying pan for 2–3 minutes, shaking the pan constantly. Grind with the peppercorns, in a mortar and pestle or clean coffee grinder, until finely ground. Wrap the shrimp paste in a small piece of foil and cook under a hot grill for 3 minutes, turning the package twice. Process the ground spices, roasted shrimp paste, nutmeg and chillies in a food processor for 5 seconds. Add the remaining ingredients and process for 20 seconds at a time, scraping down the sides of the bowl with a spatula each time, until the mixture forms a smooth paste. Refrigerate in an airtight container for up to 3 weeks.
Makes 1 1/2 cups (375 g/12 oz)

GREEN CURRY PASTE

1 tablespoon coriander seeds
2 teaspoons cumin seeds
1 teaspoon black peppercorns
2 teaspoons dried shrimp paste
8–12 large fresh green chillies, roughly chopped
4 small red chillies, roughly chopped
1 cup (110 g/3 2/3 oz) Asian shallots, chopped
5 cm (2 inches) piece of fresh galangal, pounded or chopped
12 small cloves garlic, chopped
1 cup (50 g/1 2/3 oz) chopped fresh coriander leaves, stems and roots
6 kaffir lime leaves, chopped
3 stems lemon grass (white part only), finely chopped
2 teaspoons grated lime rind
2 teaspoons salt
2 tablespoons oil

Toast the coriander and cumin seeds in a dry frying pan for 2–3 minutes, shaking the pan constantly, to prevent burning. Combine the toasted spices with the peppercorns in a mortar and pestle or clean coffee grinder and work them until they are finely ground. Wrap the shrimp paste in a small piece of foil and cook under a hot grill for 2–3 minutes, turning the package twice. Process the ground spices and shrimp paste in a food processor for 5 seconds. Add the remaining ingredients and process for 20 seconds at a time, scraping down the sides of the bowl with a spatula each time, until the mixture forms a smooth paste. Refrigerate in an airtight container for up to 3 weeks.
Makes 1 1/2 cups (375 g/12 oz)

Pastes, from left: Red Curry; Green Curry

DESSERTS

CARAMEL STICKY RICE

Preparation time: 40 minutes
+ overnight soaking
Total cooking time: 1 hour 15 minutes
Serves 4

2 cups (400 g/12⅔ oz) glutinous white rice
250 ml (8 fl oz) coconut milk
85 g (2¾ oz) palm sugar, grated
¼ teaspoon salt
starfruit, finely sliced
3 tablespoons coconut cream
1 tablespoon sesame seeds, toasted

1 Put the rice in a sieve and wash until water runs clear. Transfer to a glass or ceramic bowl and cover with water; soak overnight. Drain.

2 Line a bamboo steamer with baking paper or a damp tea towel and place it over a water-filled wok. Spread the rice over the base of the steamer, fold the sides of the paper or tea towel over the rice and then cover with another sheet of paper or tea towel; tuck it in so rice is completely encased and cover with the bamboo lid. Steam the rice over medium heat for 50 minutes, replenishing the water regularly, until just cooked.

3 Stir the coconut milk, palm sugar and salt in a small pan until boiling. Reduce the heat and simmer for 15 minutes or until the caramel is thick.

4 Pour one-quarter of the caramel over the rice, fork it through, cover again with the paper and lid and steam for 5 minutes. Repeat with the remaining caramel, cooking the rice until plump and sticky. The rice can be pressed into a square dish, left to stand and then cut into diamonds, or formed into balls and served warm. Garnish with a slice of starfruit, a drizzle of the coconut cream and some sesame seeds.

Wash the glutinous rice under running water until the water runs clear.

Grate the palm sugar on the large holes of a metal grater.

Cover the rice with baking paper, tucking in the sides to encase the rice.

Pour about one-quarter of the caramel over the steamed rice.

BANANA AND COCONUT PANCAKES

Preparation time: 20 minutes
Total cooking time: 30 minutes
Serves 4–6

1/3 cup (40 g/1 1/3 oz) plain flour
2 tablespoons rice flour
1/4 cup (60 g/2 oz) caster sugar
1/4 cup (25 g/3/4 oz) desiccated coconut
1 cup (250 ml/8 fl oz) coconut milk
1 egg, lightly beaten
4 large bananas
60 g (2 oz) butter
1/3 cup (60 g/2 oz) soft brown sugar
1/3 cup (80 ml/2 3/4 fl oz) lime juice
1 tablespoon shredded, toasted coconut, for serving
strips of lime rind, for serving

1 Sift the flours into a medium bowl. Add the sugar and coconut and mix through with a spoon. Make a well in the centre of the flour, pour in the combined coconut milk and egg and beat until smooth.
2 Heat a non-stick frying pan or crepe pan and melt a little butter in it. Pour 3 tablespoons of the pancake mixture into the pan and cook over medium heat until the underside is golden.
3 Turn the pancake over and cook the other side. Transfer to a plate and cover with a tea towel to keep warm. Repeat the process with the remaining pancake batter, buttering the pan when necessary. Keep the pancakes warm while preparing the bananas.
4 Cut the bananas diagonally into thick slices. Heat the butter in the pan; add the bananas and toss until coated. Cook over medium heat until the bananas start to soften and brown. Sprinkle with the brown sugar and shake the pan gently until the sugar has melted. Stir in the lime juice. Divide the bananas among the pancakes and fold over to enclose. Sprinkle with toasted coconut and strips of lime rind.

COOK'S FILE

Hint: These delicate pancakes are easier to turn if you slide them onto a plate and invert back into the pan.

Beat the pancake mixture thoroughly, until it is smooth.

When pancakes are cooked, transfer to a plate and keep them warm.

Toss the bananas gently until well coated with the butter.

Sprinkle brown sugar over the bananas and shake the pan until sugar dissolves.

FRUIT PLATTER

Preparation time: 25 minutes + chilling
Total cooking time: 20 minutes
Serves 4–6

1 small pineapple, peeled and chopped
1 pawpaw, peeled and chopped
3 starfruit, sliced
8 rambutans, peeled and seeded
2 cups (500 g/1 lb) caster sugar
2 cups (500 ml/16 fl oz) water
2 tablespoons lemon or lime juice
5 cm (2 inch) strip lemon or lime rind
fresh mint leaves, to garnish

1 Place the prepared fruit in a large bowl, cover and chill for at least 30 minutes.

2 Place the caster sugar and water in a medium pan. Stir over low heat, without boiling, for 5 minutes or until the sugar is dissolved. Add the juice and rind to the pan and bring the mixture to the boil. Boil, without stirring, for 10 minutes or until the syrup has thickened slightly. Remove the rind from the pan and set the mixture aside to cool.

3 Just prior to serving, pour over enough cooled syrup to coat the fruit and carefully fold it through. Arrange the fruit in an attractive bowl or hollowed out melon or on a platter. Garnish with mint leaves or sprigs.

COOK'S FILE

Storage time: The syrup can be prepared a day ahead, covered and refrigerated. However, the fruit is best prepared on the day of serving. Fruit of your choice can be added.

Peel the rambutans and use your fingers to remove the seeds.

Boil the syrup for 10 minutes, or until it thickens slightly.

Pour over enough of the cooled syrup to coat the fruit.

CASHEW MERINGUE CAKE

Preparation time: 40 minutes
+ cooling
Total cooking time: 45 minutes
Serves 8–10

Cashew Meringue
300 g (9 2/3 oz) cashews
8 egg whites
1 1/2 cups (375 g/12 oz) caster sugar
2 teaspoons vanilla essence
2 teaspoons white vinegar

Filling
250 g (8 oz) unsalted butter, softened
1 cup (125 g/4 oz) icing sugar
4 tablespoons Creme de Cacao
2 cups (500 ml/16 fl oz) cream
1 tablespoon orange liqueur
2 teaspoons vanilla essence
chocolate or cocoa, for decoration, optional

1 To make Cashew Meringue: Preheat the oven to moderate 180°C (350°F/Gas 4). Spread the cashews on a baking tray and toast them in the oven for 5 minutes or until golden, stirring occasionally to turn them over. Check frequently to make sure they don't burn. Remove from the oven, allow to cool and then process in short bursts in a food processor, until finely ground. Reduce the oven temperature to slow 150°C (300°/Gas 2). Line 4 oven trays with non-stick baking paper and draw a 21 cm (8 1/2 inch) diameter circle onto each piece of paper.

2 Beat the egg whites in a large, clean, dry bowl until soft peaks form. Gradually add the caster sugar to the bowl, beating well after each addition, until the whites are thick and glossy. Using a metal spoon, fold in the vanilla, vinegar and ground cashews.

3 Divide the mixture evenly among the circles and carefully spread it to the edge of each circle. Bake the meringues for 45 minutes or until they are crisp. Turn the oven off and allow the meringues to cool in the oven, leaving the oven door ajar.

4 To make Filling: In a medium bowl, beat the butter, icing sugar and Creme de Cacao until the mixture is light and creamy. Set aside. In a separate bowl, beat the cream, orange liqueur and vanilla essence, until soft peaks form.

5 Place 1 meringue circle on a serving plate and carefully spread with half of the Creme de Cacao mixture. Top with another meringue circle and spread with half of the orange cream mixture. Repeat with the remaining meringue circles, Creme de Cacao mixture and orange cream mixture.

6 The top of the meringue cake can be decorated with chocolate curls and dusted lightly with cocoa. Carefully cut into sections for serving.

COOK'S FILE

Variation: The cashew nuts can be replaced with almonds, pecans or hazelnuts.

Hint: If your oven doesn't have four racks, cook two meringue circles at a time.

Note: This cake, known as *Sansrival*, is a celebration cake always served at fiestas and special occasions in the Philippines. The cream filling may vary in each village.

Process the roasted cashews, after they have cooled, until finely ground.

Using a plate as a guide, draw a circle onto each piece of paper.

Fold the vanilla essence, vinegar and ground cashews into the egg whites.

Use a spatula to spread the meringue mixture to the edge of each circle.

Beat the butter, icing sugar and Creme de Cacao until light and creamy.

Spread the second layer of meringue with half the orange cream.

FRESH MANGO ICE CREAM

Preparation time: 20 minutes + freezing
Total cooking time: Nil
Makes approximately 900 ml (approximately 30 fl oz)

3 fresh mangoes (approximately 1.5 kg/3 lb)
1/2 cup (125 g/4 oz) caster sugar
3 tablespoons mango nectar
300 ml (9 1/2 fl oz) cream

1 Peel the mangoes, cut into pieces and purée in a food processor until smooth. Transfer to a bowl and add the sugar and nectar. Stir until the sugar has dissolved.
2 Beat the cream in a small bowl until stiff peaks form and then gently fold it through the mango mixture.
3 Spoon the mixture into a shallow rectangular tray, cover and freeze for 1 1/2 hours or until half-frozen. Quickly spoon the mixture into a food processor and process for 30 seconds, or until smooth. Return the mixture to the tray or a plastic container, cover and freeze completely. Remove the ice cream from the freezer 15 minutes before serving, to allow it to soften a little. Serve in scoops with some extra, fresh mango, if you wish.

COOK'S FILE

Storage time: Freeze the ice cream for at least eight hours — it can be frozen for up to three weeks.
Variation: Stir in some toasted, desiccated coconut before freezing the ice cream completely.

Process the mangoes in a food processor until smooth.

Fold the whipped cream through the mango mixture.

Pour the processed ice cream back into the tray and freeze completely.

STICKY BLACK RICE

Preparation time: 20 minutes + overnight soaking
Total cooking time: 40 minutes
Serves 6–8

2 cups (400 g/12 2/3 oz) black rice
1 litre cold water
2 cups (500 ml/16 fl oz) coconut milk
80 g (2 2/3 oz) palm sugar, grated
3 tablespoons caster sugar
3 fresh pandan leaves, shredded and knotted
3 tablespoons coconut cream
3 tablespoons creamed corn

1 Place the rice in a large glass or ceramic bowl and cover with water. Soak for at least 8 hours or overnight. Drain and transfer to a medium pan with the 1 litre of water. Bring slowly to the boil, stirring frequently, and simmer for 20 minutes, or until tender. Drain.
2 In a large heavy-based pan, heat the coconut milk until almost boiling. Add the palm sugar, caster sugar and pandan leaves and stir until dissolved. Add the rice and stir for 3–4 minutes without boiling.

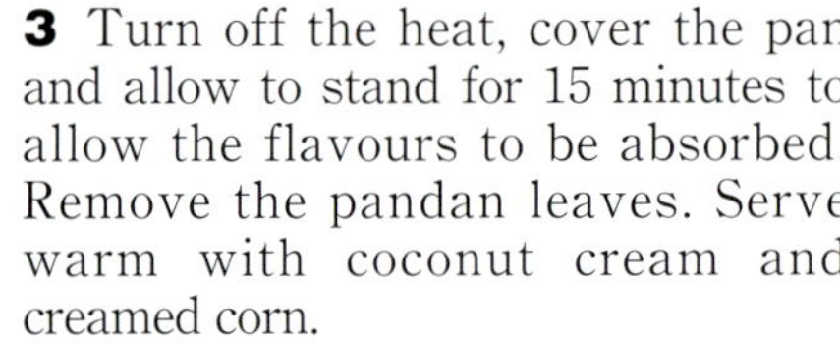

3 Turn off the heat, cover the pan and allow to stand for 15 minutes to allow the flavours to be absorbed. Remove the pandan leaves. Serve warm with coconut cream and creamed corn.

COOK'S FILE

Notes: Black rice, palm sugar and pandan leaves are all available from Asian food speciality stores.
- Creamed corn is traditionally served with coconut cream and sticky rice.
- One teaspoon of pandan essence or vanilla essence can be used if fresh pandan leaves are not available.

Soak the black rice in water for at least 8 hours, or overnight.

Add the palm sugar, caster sugar and pandan leaves to the coconut milk.

Use tongs to remove the pandan leaves from the mixture.

Fresh Mango Ice Cream (top) and Sticky Black Rice

SAGO PUDDING

Preparation time: 20 minutes
+ 1 hour soaking
+ 2 hours refrigeration
Total cooking time: 20 minutes
Serves 6

1 cup (195 g/6 1/3 oz) sago
3 cups (750 ml/24 fl oz) water
1 cup (185 g/6 oz) soft brown sugar
1 cup (250 ml/8 fl oz) water, extra
1 cup (250 ml/8 fl oz) coconut cream, well chilled

1 Soak the sago in the 3 cups of water for 1 hour. Pour into a medium pan, add 2 tablespoons of the brown sugar and bring to the boil over low heat, stirring constantly. Reduce the heat and simmer, stirring occasionally, for 10 minutes. Cover and cook over low heat, stirring occasionally, for 2–3 minutes, until the mixture becomes thick and sago grains are translucent.
2 Half fill six rinsed (still wet) 1/2-cup moulds with the sago mixture. Refrigerate for 2 hours, or until set.
3 Combine the remaining brown sugar with the extra water in a small pan and cook over low heat, stirring constantly, until the sugar dissolves. Simmer for 5–7 minutes, until the syrup thickens. Remove from the heat and cool. To serve, the sago can be unmoulded, if desired, and topped with a little of the sugar syrup and coconut cream.

COOK'S FILE

Note: Palm sugar can be used instead of brown sugar — grate it on a cheese grater, or shred with a sharp knife, before using.
Storage time: The syrup can be made up to a day in advance, covered and refrigerated.

Stir the sago constantly, over low heat, until boiling.

Cook until the mixture thickens and the sago grains are translucent.

Simmer the syrup for 5–7 minutes, until it thickens.

INDEX

INTERNATIONAL GLOSSARY OF INGREDIENTS OR ALTERNATIVES

Asian shallot	can use French shallot
baby spinach leaves	baby English spinach leaves
baby squash	pattypan squash
bok choy	pak choi, pak choy
calamari	squid
capsicum	red or green pepper
caster sugar	superfine sugar
chickpea	garbanzo beans
chilli	chile/chili pepper
cornflour	cornstarch
cream	single/light whipping cream
eggplant	aubergine
English spinach	spinach
fresh coriander	fresh cilantro
Hokkien noodle	egg noodle
icing sugar	confectioners' sugar
Lebanese cucumber	short cucumber
mince	ground meat
plain flour	all-purpose flour
prawn, raw	shrimp, green
snow pea	mangetout
soft brown sugar	light brown sugar
spring onion	scallion
telegraph cucumber	long cucumber
Thai basil	can use any basil
thick cream	double/heavy cream
Vietnamese mint	can use any mint
zucchini	courgette

This edition published in 2003 by Bay Books, an imprint of Murdoch Magazines Pty Limited, GPO Box 1203, Sydney NSW 2001, Australia.

Managing Editor: Rachel Carter **Editor:** Wendy Stephen
Food Director: Jane Lawson **Food Editors:** Kerrie Ray, Tracy Rutherford, Jody Vassallo
Designer: Wing Ping Tong **Recipe Development:** Jo Richardson, Jody Vassallo
Home Economists: Michelle Lawton, Jo Richardson, Alison Turner
Photographers: Joe Filshie, Reg Morrison (steps)
Food Stylist: Donna Hay **Food Preparation:** Alison Turner
Chief Executive: Juliet Rogers. **Publisher:** Kay Scarlett.

ISBN 0 86411 547 4.
Reprinted 2004. Printed by Sing Cheong Printing Co. Ltd. PRINTED IN CHINA.
Copyright© Text, design, photography and illustrations Murdoch Books® 1997. All rights reserved.
No part of this publication may be reproduced, stored in a retrieval system or transmitted in any form or by any means, electronic,mechanical, photocopying, recording or otherwise without the prior written permission of the publisher.
Murdoch Books® is a registered trademark of Murdoch Magazines Pty Ltd.